JERUSALEM

Jerusalem

HENRY CATTAN

ST. MARTIN'S PRESS NEW YORK

Library of Congress Cataloguing in Publication Data

Cattan, Henry.
   Jerusalem.

   Includes bibliographical references and index.
   1. Jerusalem–History.   2. Jerusalem–Politics and government.
   I. Title.

   DS109.9.C37   1981   956.94'4   80-21235
   ISBN 0-312-44182-7

CONTENTS

List of Appendices

1. The Problem of Jerusalem 9

2. Jerusalem from Early Times until 1917 17

3. British Occupation and Mandate, 1917-1948 31

4. The Battle for Jerusalem, 1948 41

5. Jerusalem between 1948 and 1967 53

6. Israel's Capture of the Old City, 1967, and its Aftermath 67

7. The Massive Colonization of Jerusalem and its Surroundings 79

8. The Judaization of Jerusalem: Its Significance and Perils 91

9. International Legal Status of Jerusalem 101

10. Nullity of Israel's Actions in Jerusalem 119

11. Whether Resolution 242 or Partition Offers a
    Satisfactory Solution 127

12. Obstacles to a Solution 135

13. Conservatory Measures Pending Final Settlement 141

Appendices 153

Postscript 221

Index 225

APPENDICES*

I   Chronology of Jerusalem

II   Christian Holy Places and religious shrines in Jerusalem and its vicinity

III   Moslem Holy Places and religious shrines in Jerusalem and its vicinity

IV   Jewish Holy Places and religious shrines in Jerusalem and its vicinity

V   Municipal map of Jerusalem showing Arab and Jewish quarters in 1948

VI   Schedule of Arab and Jewish land ownership in Jerusalem in 1948

VII Excerpts from General Assembly resolution 181 (II) of 29 November 1947 concerning the future government of Palestine and the internationalization of Jerusalem

VIII Map of *corpus separatum* of Jerusalem in accordance with General Assembly resolution 181 (II) of 29 November 1947

IX   Resolution 194 (III) of the General Assembly dated 11 December 1948 concerning the Conciliation Commission, the international régime of Jerusalem and the return of refugees

X   Resolution 273 (III) of the General Assembly dated 11 May 1949 concerning the admission of Israel to UN membership

XI   Resolution 303 (IV) of the General Assembly dated 9 December 1949 concerning the international régime for Jerusalem

*The Appendices set out at the end of this book include all relevant UN resolutions pertaining solely to Jerusalem. There exist a number of other resolutions concerning refugees, the inalienable rights of the people of Palestine and Israeli practices, policies and violations of human rights which are omitted because of considerations of space.

XII	Resolution 2253 (ES-V) of the General Assembly dated 4 July 1967 concerning measures taken by Israel to change the status of Jerusalem
XIII	Resolution 2254 (ES-V) of the General Assembly dated 14 July 1967 concerning measures taken by Israel to change the status of Jerusalem
XIV	Resolution 242 of the Security Council dated 22 November 1967 concerning withdrawal of Israeli armed forces and termination of belligerency
XV	Resolution 252 of the Security Council dated 21 May 1968 concerning measures taken by Israel to change the legal status of Jerusalem
XVI	Resolution 267 of the Security Council dated 3 July 1969 concerning measures taken by Israel to change the status of Jerusalem
XVII	Resolution 271 of the Security Council dated 15 September 1969 concerning arson at Al-Aqsa Mosque and measures taken by Israel to change the status of Jerusalem
XVIII	Resolution 298 of the Security Council dated 25 September 1971 concerning measures taken by Israel to change the status of Jerusalem
XIX	Excerpts from resolution 2851 (XXVI) of the General Assembly dated 20 December 1971 concerning violations by Israel of human rights in the occupied territories
XX	Excerpts from resolution of the Commission on Human Rights of the Economic and Social Council of the UN dated 11 February 1974 condemning Israel's policy of annexation and transfer of population in the occupied territories, including Jerusalem
XXI	Excerpts from resolution of the Commission on Human Rights of the Economic and Social Council of the UN dated 21 February 1975 condemning Israel's violations of human rights in the occupied territories and censuring Israel's acts in Jerusalem
XXII	Excerpts from resolutions 31/106 A and C adopted by the General Assembly on 16 December 1976 concerning the occupied territories, including Jerusalem
XXIII	Excerpts from resolution 1 (XXXIII) A adopted by the Commission on Human Rights on 15 February 1977 regarding violations of human rights in the occupied territories, including Jerusalem
XXIV	Excerpts from resolution 32/5 adopted by the General Assembly on 28 October 1977 regarding illegal Israeli

measures designed to change the legal status, geographical
nature and demographic composition of the occupied
territories, including Jerusalem

XXV   Excerpts from resolutions 32/91 A and C adopted by
the General Assembly on 13 December 1977 reaffirming
the applicability of the Geneva Convention of 12
August 1949 to, and condemning Israeli policies and
practices in, the occupied territories, including Jerusalem

XXVI   Excerpts from resolution of the General Conference of
the UN Educational, Scientific and Cultural Organization
(UNESCO) of 28 November 1978 condemning the
judaization by Israel of the historic and cultural
configuration of Jerusalem

XXVII   Excerpts from resolutions 33/113 A, B and C of the
General Assembly of 18 December 1978 reaffirming
the nullity of the measures taken by Israel in Jerusalem

XXVIII   Excerpts from resolution 1 (XXXV) of the Commission
on Human Rights of the Economic and Social Council
of the UN dated 21 February 1979 condemning Israel's
violations of human rights in the occupied territories
and reaffirming the applicability of the Geneva
Convention to such territories, including Jerusalem

XXIX   Resolution 446 of the Security Council dated 22 March
1979 calling upon Israel to rescind measures taken to
change the legal status, geographical nature and demographic composition of Arab territories, including
Jerusalem

XXX   Resolution 452 of the Security Council dated 20 July
1979 calling upon Israel to cease the establishment of
settlements in occupied territories, including Jerusalem

XXXI   Excerpts from resolution 34/70 of the General Assembly
of 6 December 1979 declaring that a just and lasting
settlement must be based on attainment by the Palestinian
people of its inalienable rights and Israeli withdrawal
from all occupied territories, including Jerusalem

XXXII   Excerpts from resolutions 1 A and B (XXXVI) of the
Commission on Human Rights of the Economic and Social
Council of the UN dated 13 February 1980 on the violations
of human rights in the occupied territories, including
Jerusalem

XXXIII   Resolution 465 of the Security Council dated 1 March
1980 calling upon Israel to cease the establishment of
settlements and to dismantle existing settlements in
occupied territories, including Jerusalem

XXXIV   Resolution 476 (1980) of the Security Council adopted on

30 June 1980 reconfirming that all legislative and administrative measures taken by Israel which purport to alter the character and status of the Holy City of Jerusalem have no legal validity

XXXV Resolution ES/72 (1980) adopted by the General Assembly on 29 July 1980 requiring Israel to withdraw from all territories occupied in 1967, including Jerusalem

XXXVI Resolution 478 adopted by the Security Council on 20 August 1980 which censured the enactment by Israel of a basic law proclaiming a change in the character and status of Jerusalem and declared it null and void

Chapter One

THE PROBLEM OF JERUSALEM

Religious Significance of Jerusalem

The problem of Jerusalem is one of the most emotional and explosive issues in the world. Unlike other issues of the Arab-Israeli conflict, its importance and dimensions transcend the Middle East and its peoples.

Jerusalem is unique among all the cities of the world because of its association with three religions. It is the spiritual and religious heritage to one half of humanity and is holy for one thousand million Christians, seven hundred million Moslems and fourteen million Jews.

Jerusalem is the birthplace of Christianity. Almost all the Holy Places, sacred shrines and sanctuaries connected with the birth, life and death of Christ are found in Jerusalem and in nearby Bethlehem: the Holy Sepulchre, the Via Dolorosa, the Church of the Nativity, the Cenacle, the Garden of Gethsemane, the Mount of Olives and thirty-eight churches.[1]

Jerusalem is also holy for Islam:

> All Islamic traditions and sacred writings point to the unmistakable fact that Jerusalem is holy for all Moslems, second only in holiness to Mecca and Medina. It is the *qibla* (direction for prayer) and the third of the sacred cities.[2]

The name of Jerusalem in Arabic is '*Al Qods*' which means 'The Holy'.

On the site of the *Haram Al-Sharif* in the Old City of Jerusalem stand two famous Islamic sanctuaries: the Mosque of the Dome of the Rock which was built in the seventh century and is associated, in accordance with Islamic tradition, with the Prophet's ascension to heaven during his Night Journey, and the Mosque of Al-Aqsa, meaning 'the farthest', which was built in the eighth century on the place associated by Islamic tradition with 'the farthest Mosque' mentioned in the Qur'an (*surah* xvii:1).[3]

In addition to these two historic mosques, there exist thirty-four other mosques in Jerusalem, twenty-seven of which are located in the Old City and the others outside the walls.[4]

To Judaism, Jerusalem has been a holy city since the building of the

Temple of Solomon. This Temple, completed in 962 BC, was destroyed
by the Babylonians in 587 BC. A second Temple of a humble character
was built around 515 BC after the return of the Jews from captivity
but was again destroyed by the Macedonians in 170 BC. It was reconstructed in Herod's time only to be destroyed for a third time by the
Romans following the Jewish insurrection in AD 70. Today the most
important Jewish sanctuary in Jerusalem is the Wailing Wall which the
Jews consider to be the remnant of the western wall of Herod's Temple.[5]

The significance of Jerusalem, however, does not lie merely in the
Holy Places and sanctuaries of the three great religions. In addition all
three have a vital interest in preserving the living presence of the adherents to their faith in the Holy City.[6]

Jerusalem has been the scene of many dramatic events and the cause
of many wars during the thirty-eight centuries of its known existence.
It has suffered more than twenty sieges, changed hands more than
twenty-five times, was destroyed seventeen times, and its inhabitants
were massacred on several occasions. The last act in the drama of
Jerusalem occurred in our lifetime. Under the pretext that the city was
the capital of a Jewish kingdom in biblical times about thirty centuries
ago, Zionist Jews, who had come to Palestine as immigrants during the
British mandate, established in 1948 the State of Israel, seized and
usurped Jerusalem and displaced and dispossessed most of its original
inhabitants.

Zionism

The upheaval which occurred in Jerusalem is attributable to Zionism
and its political ambitions. The question may be asked, what is Zionism?

Since the destruction of the Temple and the deportation of the Jews
by the Romans in AD 135 following their second revolt, religious Jews
have prayed for their return to Zion. This religious and mystical attachment did not involve any political, territorial or nationalist aims and
ambitions. In fact, very few Jews returned to Jerusalem for many centuries. On the other hand, the Jewish religious attachment to Jerusalem
did not cause any concern among the Arabs of Palestine or elsewhere
who always had shown tolerance and hospitality to those Jews seeking
refuge in Arab countries to escape from persecution in Europe. It was
the Arab rulers who abolished the prohibition on the presence of Jews
in Jerusalem which had been imposed by Emperor Hadrian in AD 135
and renewed by his successors before the capture of the city by the

Moslem Arabs.

In the nineteenth century, as a result of anti-semitism, persecution and the rise of nationalism, some new currents of thought developed among European Jews regarding Palestine. Some of these currents of thought were purely spiritual and cultural, others nationalistic. The latter found expression in the concept for the creation of a Jewish state and became known as Zionism. The author of this concept was Theodor Herzl, an Austrian journalist, who published in 1896 a pamphlet *Der Judenstaat* (The Jewish State) in which he advocated Jewish colonization in Argentina or Palestine with a view to the creation of a Jewish state. Herzl's concern was to find a solution to the problem of anti-semitism, not the fulfilment of biblical prophecies.[7] This is borne out by his proposal of Argentina as an alternative to Palestine for Jewish colonization and the eventual creation of a Jewish state. Herzl even considered the acceptance of a territory in East Africa which was offered to him by the British Government for Jewish colonization. But at the first Zionist Congress which he convened in 1897 at Basle, the religious trend prevailed and the aim of Zionism was proclaimed to be the creation of a 'home' for the Jewish people in Palestine.

To the extent that the concept of a Jewish home in Palestine involved the establishment of a secular state, it did not command the general approval of Jewry or even of all Zionists. Ronald Storrs, first Governor of Jerusalem in the early days of the British administration in Palestine, states: 'The religious Jews of Jerusalem and Hebron and the *Sephardim* were strongly opposed to political Zionism, holding that God would bring Israel back to Zion in His own good time, and that it was impious to anticipate His decree.'[8] Commenting upon the secular orientation of Zionism towards the creation of a Jewish state, Professor Norton Mezvinsky states:

> Serious differences arose among those Jews who were committed Zionists. In their expressions of so-called 'spiritual' or 'cultural' Zionism, for example, Asher Ginsburg (1886-1927), commonly known by his pseudonym Ahad Haam, Martin Buber (1878-1969), and others stood in opposition to political Zionism. Expressing far more concern about the 'Arab inhabitants' of Palestine who were not Jews and being more interested in a Jewish cultural rather than religious renaissance, many of these people opted at times to advocate something other than a Jewish nation-state in Palestine; they rather favored a spiritual-cultural center in Palestine for Jews. But such advocacy was trampled asunder within the Zionism movement.[9]

The Zionist concept gained a certain measure of international support by the declaration issued by the British Government on 2 November 1917 in the letter to Lord Balfour which viewed with favour the establishment of a Jewish national home in Palestine and by the incorporation of such declaration in the mandate granted in 1922 by the League of Nations to Great Britain to administer Palestine.

In 1948 Zionism realized its dream of statehood by the proclamation by 'the Jewish people in Palestine and the World Zionist Movement' of a Jewish state which they called Israel. The proclamation was purportedly made on the basis of resolution 181 (II) of the General Assembly of the UN dated 29 November 1947 which had recommended the termination of the British mandate over Palestine, the creation of Arab and Jewish states and the establishment of a special international régime for Jerusalem.

Evolution of Zionism

The concept of Zionism which was originally innocuous in character had become over the years a mixture of nationalism, idealism and mysticism. But from the time of the establishment of the State of Israel, the concept of Zionism underwent a profound and radical change. It became an increasingly racist concept having as its objective the exclusivist Jewishness of the people and the land in the new state. This required the obliteration of Palestine, its history and its people.

The Zionist objective was realized in Palestine by the seizure of the country, partly in 1948 and completely in 1967, by the displacement of one million people in 1948 and 400,000 in 1967, that is, two-thirds of the population who became and still are refugees, by the refusal of all UN efforts to secure their repatriation and by the bringing into the country of over two and a half million Jewish settlers who were given the homes and lands of the Palestinians.

In Jerusalem the Zionist objective was realized by the capture and annexation first of its modern section and then of the Old City, the displacement of most of its original Arab inhabitants, its judaization and colonization with some two hundred thousand Jewish settlers.

The racism of Israel — vehemently denied by Israel and its friends — is indubitably established by the facts. It is not denied by Jewish observers.[10] Maxime Rodinson observes that the Jewish character of the state is 'the prime aim and postulate of Zionist ideology'.[11] Nahum Goldmann, former President of the World Zionist Organization, has been critical of Israel's policies in regard to the Palestinians, accusing it of 'a radical distortion of the Zionist ideal'.[12] In a resolution adopted on 10 November 1975 the General Assembly of the UN proclaimed that Zionism is a form of racism and racial discrimination.

The policy pursued by Israel since its creation of obliterating the name and history of Palestine, of effacing the Palestinian physical presence and judaizing Jerusalem could lead, if one rightly construes the Israeli threats against, and desecration or vandalism of, non-Jewish Holy Places, to the obliteration sooner or later of the Islamic and Christian religious heritage in Jerusalem. Neither the Palestinians, nor the Arabs, nor Islam and Christianity will acquiesce in this Israeli domination and judaization of Jerusalem.

This is the problem of Jerusalem which will be more fully discussed in the following pages.

Notes

1. A list of Christian Holy Places and religious shrines in Jerusalem is given in Appendix II.

2. H.S. Karmi, 'How Holy is Palestine to the Muslims?', *Islamic Quarterly Magazine*, Vol. 14, No. 2 (1970), p. 69.

3. *Surah* xvii:1 states: 'Glory to [God] Who did take His Servant for a journey by night from the Sacred Mosque to the Farthest Mosque, whose precincts We did bless, in order that We might show him some of Our Signs: for He is the One who heareth and seeth [all things].'

4. For a description of these mosques, see Aref Al Aref, *A History of Jerusalem* (Arabic) (Andalus Library, Jerusalem, 1961). A list of Moslem Holy Places and religious shrines in Jerusalem is given in Appendix III.

5. A list of Jewish Holy Places and religious shrines in Jerusalem is given in Appendix IV.

6. Following the upheaval of 1948, Rev. Charles T. Bridgeman expressed concern over the fate of the Christians in Jerusalem in his letter to the President of the Trusteeship Council dated 13 January 1950 (Supp. No. 9, A/1286, p. 17) in these terms:

> The real Christian stake in the Holy City lies in the lives of the 31,000 Christians who normally inhabit the city and constitute the oldest Christian community in the world.
>
> The attempt has been made to becloud this fact by speaking as though the only interest Christians had in the Holy City lay in a few Holy Places . . .
>
> But still more important to every Christian community is the wholesome life of its members and the continuance of the Christian community as a vital part of the complex life in the Holy City.
>
> At the present moment the vast majority of the Christians are refugees from their homes, their businesses, their churches, their schools and their hospitals, and if under a partitioned Jerusalem they are prohibited from repossessing the homes now occupied by new immigrants they will have been permanently dispossessed of their stake in the Holy City.

7. F.F. Andrews, *The Holy Land under Mandate*, Vol. 1 (Houghton and Mifflin, New York, 1931), p. 303.

8. Ronald Storrs, *Orientations* (Nicholson and Watson, London, 1945), p. 340. The *Sephardim* are the Oriental Jews in contradistinction to the *Ashkenazim* or European Jews.

9. N. Mezvinsky, 'The Jewish Faith and the Problem of Israel and Jerusalem', International Seminar on Jerusalem, London, December 1979.

10. The racist policy and practices of Israel were exposed by Dr Israel Shahak, Professor at the Hebrew University of Jerusalem and President of the Israeli League for Human Rights in his book *Le Racisme de l'Etat d'Israel* (Guy Authier, Paris, 1975) in which he denounces torture and repression of the Arabs, destruction of 385 Arab villages, persecution and racial discrimination.

11. Maxime Rodinson, *Israel and the Arabs* (Penguin, Harmondsworth, 1968), p. 228.

12. Nahum Goldmann, 'Zionist Ideology and the Reality of Israel', *Foreign Affairs* (Fall 1978), p. 70. See also by the same author: *The Jewish Paradox* (Weidenfeld and Nicolson, London, 1978) and *Où Va Israël* (Calman-Levy, Paris, 1975).

Chapter Two

JERUSALEM FROM EARLY TIMES UNTIL 1917

Canaanite Period (1800-1000 BC)

It is obvious that only a broad and schematic outline of the history of Jerusalem which covers a span of at least thirty-eight centuries can be attempted in this chapter. Such an outline, however succinct, is necessary for understanding the question of Jerusalem as it presents itself today. The roots of the problem do not only lie in recent developments, but extend back centuries far deep into the distant past. It is imperative, when Israel seeks to justify its capture and annexation of Jerusalem on the ground that it was the capital of a Jewish kingdom some three thousand years ago, to examine, in its proper perspective, the role which the Jews have played in the history of the city.

The history of Jerusalem in the two millennia until David's time remains poorly documented, but just after the second millennium the veil is lifted to give a brief, though illuminating, glimpse into Jerusalem's obscurity.[1] During the last decade archaeology has dug up some important facts of the history of Jerusalem.

Jerusalem is one of the oldest cities in the world. According to Josephus who wrote in the first century of our era, it was founded by the Canaanites. Josephus wrote:

> But he who first built it [Jerusalem] was a potent man among the Canaanites, and is in our tongue called Melchisedek, *The Righteous King*, for such he really was; on which account he was [there] the first priest of God, and first built a temple [there], and called the city Jerusalem, which was formerly called Salem.[2]

As to the date of the founding of Jerusalem, if one accepts the statement of Josephus that its founder was Melchisedek and since the latter was a contemporary of Abraham (Genesis 14:18), this would date the founding of Jerusalem to over eighteen centuries BC. The city was, therefore, already in existence several centuries before the arrival of the Israelites to the land of Canaan (as Palestine was then called) about 1200 BC, or its capture by David in or around 1000 BC. In fact, the Jewish Encyclopedia mentions that in Hebrew annals 'Jerusalem is expressly called a "foreign city" not belonging to the Israelites (Judges 19:12), and the Jebusites are said to have lived there for very many years together with the Benjamites'.[3]

Without ascribing any particular date to the founding of Jerusalem, Father R.de Vaux, an eminent archaeologist, states that about 1800 to 1550 BC, Jerusalem was one of several cities protected by ramparts which sprang up in Palestine.[4]

It seems necessary to stress the fact that Jerusalem was founded by the Canaanites long before its capture by David because some present-day Israeli politicians falsely claim that it was founded by the Jews. Thus at the time of the capture of the Old City of Jerusalem in June 1967, Ygal Allon, then Israel's Deputy Prime Minister, was reported by the press to have said: 'The world must reconcile itself to the fact that the city has at last returned to the nation that founded it and turned it into a Holy City' when, in fact, Jerusalem existed as a Canaanite sacred city for several hundred years before the Israelites set foot in Palestine.

Recent excavations have confirmed the early founding of Jerusalem. In 1961 excavations by the British School of Archaeology in Jerusalem showed that a walled town existed on part of the site during the Middle Bronze Age II, probably in 1800 BC. Clearly, therefore, before the arrival of the Israelites, Jerusalem was a 'Canaanite city of importance.'[5] Archaeologist Kathleen Kenyon even suggests that there was a Jerusalem in the third millennium BC.[6] The fact that Jerusalem existed long before the arrival of the Israelites is further borne out by its vassalage at a period of its history to the Pharaohs of Egypt. The Tell El-Amarna Tablets, which were discovered in 1887 but date back to the fourteenth century BC, embody appeals made to the Pharaoh of Egypt by the King of the city — then called *Urusalim* — for assistance against invaders. In fact, Jerusalem was under the overlordship of the Pharaohs between the fifteenth and the twelfth centuries BC.

Jerusalem was inhabited by the Jebusites, a Canaanite sub-group. It was one of the oldest and most illustrious royal cities in the country[7] and for some 800 years it remained a purely Canaanite city.

The Canaanites are the earliest known inhabitants of Palestine and are thought to have settled in this country at about 3000 BC. The Canaanites lived in cities as a settled population and possessed an economy based upon agriculture and commerce. Each city was ruled by a king who also performed the functions of a high priest. Not much is known about the religion of the Canaanites. In a country divided into a number of small states, it is doubtful that they possessed a unified religion, like Egypt or Mesopotamia, and each city possessed its favourite gods, its rituals and its sacred legends.[8]

The Canaanites gave to Palestine its early name, for the Bible refers to it as 'the land of Canaan' (Numbers 34:1, 35:10). It was the Philistines, however, who gave the country its present name of Palestine. The Philistines, who were called 'The People of the Sea', are thought to have come from Illyria to the land of Canaan about 1175 BC and occupied its southern coast and the maritime plain to a point north of Japho (Jaffa). The Philistines and the Canaanites are the ancestors of the Palestinians of today.[9] The Canaanites ruled Jerusalem until the eve of the first millennium BC when it was captured by the Israelites.

Israelite Period (1000-587 BC)

After their exodus from Egypt, the Israelites reached the land of Canaan in about 1200 BC. They entered it from the east and slowly spread into the heart of the country where they settled as the Twelve Tribes of Israel. According to modern historians, and contrary to a belief engendered by certain passages in the Bible, the Israelites did not massacre the Canaanite population or destroy their cities, but settled at first in unoccupied regions. Then they progressively moved into the interior. The process of Israelite settlement was slow for Jerusalem 'remained a Canaanite enclave for a further two centuries'.[10] John Gray mentions that even when the territory of the city-state was occupied 'the city itself remained in possession of its pre-Israelite inhabitants, being only reduced under David'.[11]

The Twelve Tribes of Israel were ruled by the Judges. However, the need to co-ordinate their military forces in their continual wars against the Philistines, who lived in the south and along the coast, led to the pre-eminence of Saul who was proclaimed in 1030 BC King of the Israelites. Saul was slain by the Philistines at the battle of Gilboa around 1010 BC. After Saul's death, David, who had ruled Hebron as a vassal of the Philistines, threw up their overlordship, united the Israeli Tribes and succeeded Saul as the King of the Jews.[12]

David distinguished himself by his military exploits. In or about the year 1000 BC, David laid siege to Jerusalem and captured it from the Jebusites after entering it through a water canal.

Having captured the city, David made it the capital of his kingdom. Explaining the reason that led David to move the capital of his kingdom from Hebron to Jerusalem, F.F. Bruce says:

Politically it was admirably adapted to be his royal city, for it was neither Israelite nor Judean, and neither Israel nor Judah could complain that the other was favoured in this respect. It remained a city-state in its own right, governed by the King of Israel and Judah, who now succeeded to its ancient dynasty of priest-kings. A sacred city of such ancient prestige was a worthy capital for the founder of a new dynasty under which all elements in the population of Canaan were to be united; it had venerable associations in Israelite as well as in Canaanite eyes, for did not Melchisedek, priest of 'El Elyon, come forth from there to greet Abraham when the patriarch returned from the rout of the invading kings from the east'?[13]

After taking Jerusalem, 'David dwelt in the fort and called it the city of David' (2 Samuel 5:9). According to the classical custom of the time, a captured town was given the name of its conqueror.[14] The Bible, however, contains a reminder to the city's new occupiers of its non-Jewish origin:

And say, Thus saith the Lord God unto Jerusalem: Thy birth and Thy nativity is of the land of Canaan; Thy father was an Amorite, and Thy mother an Hittite (Ezekiel 16:3).

It is appropriate to mention one important fact concerning David's capture of Jerusalem which stands in contrast to what happened thirty centuries later. He did not displace and dispossess its original inhabitants: the Jebusites were allowed to remain in their city, but not in the fortress, he (David) permitted them to settle in the east of the town, on Mount Moriah.[15] The continued existence of non-Israelites in the new Jewish kingdom is further confirmed by the Bible which refers to the people whom the children of Israel were not able to destroy and upon whom Solomon levied a tribute of bondservice (1 Kings 9:20-1).

David ruled Jerusalem for thirty-three years, and after his death his son Solomon ruled it for forty years. During Solomon's reign peace prevailed and he ordered the construction at Jerusalem of the Temple with which his name has been associated. The building of the Temple started in 969 BC and was completed in 962 BC.

Shortly after Solomon's death, the Israeli Tribes revolted and the unified kingdom established by David was split into the Kingdom of Israel in the north which was formed by ten of the Twelve Tribes, and the Kingdom of Judah in the south, with Jerusalem as its capital, which was formed by the Tribes of Judah and Benjamin. The unified kingdom established by David had lasted only seventy-three years. The dream of a unified Jewish kingdom in Palestine was thus shattered and the two new Jewish kingdoms were almost continually engaged in war between themselves or with neighbouring peoples. The Kingdom of Israel, however, did not survive long because in 733 BC the Assyrians overran its territories and in 721 BC it completely ceased to exist.

As to the 'pseudo-autonomous' Kingdom of Judah, as called by K. Kenyon, it survived for a while but led a precarious existence. Its capital, Jerusalem, was periodically besieged, taken and sacked by the Philistines, the Arabs, the Syrians, the Babylonians and the Egyptians,[16] and for long periods of time it paid tribute to Egypt and Babylon. In 587 BC the Babylonians under Nebuchadnezzar attacked and destroyed Jerusalem, burned the Temple and carried its inhabitants into captivity at Babylon where they were absorbed into their new surroundings. This represented the end of the Kingdom of Judah.

Pagan Period (587 BC to AD 323)

After its capture by the Babylonians and except for the period of the revolt by the Maccabees, Jerusalem was ruled for the following nine centuries by pagans. It was ruled first by Babylon from 587 to 538 BC when it was captured by Cyrus, King of Persia, who issued his famous edict allowing the Jews who had been deported to Babylon to return to Palestine and to rebuild the Temple. Only a small number, however, returned as the majority chose to remain in Babylon where they had settled down.[17]

Jerusalem remained in the hands of the Persians during the two following centuries until it was wrested from them in 332 BC by Alexander the Great. The Greeks held Jerusalem for a century and a half but in 167 BC the Maccabees revolted against their Greek rulers because they had prohibited the Jewish faith and converted the Jewish Temple to a temple for Jupiter. Although the Maccabees succeeded in liberating a part of Jerusalem, the Greek garrison continued to hold the citadel. This curious situation of the Greek garrison besieging the Jews in the Temple and the Jews besieging the Greeks in the citadel continued until 141 BC when Simon Maccabaeus finally reduced the Greek garrison.

Maccabean independence, however, did not last because in 134 BC Jerusalem was besieged by Antiochus Sidetes, King of Syria, and the siege was raised only upon the payment of a tribute. Seventy years later in 63 BC Pompey captured Jerusalem for Rome and put an end to Jewish rule in the city which had lasted less than eighty years in all.

In 40 BC the Romans set up Herod, who was an Idumaean and had helped the Romans, as a vassal king and Palestine became the Roman province of Judea. Herod reconstructed the Temple in a more sumptuous manner than had been done in 515 BC. On his death in 4 BC he was succeeded by his son who was deposed by the Romans two years later and Jerusalem was then governed by a Roman procurator.

It was during the Roman era that one of the momentous events in the history of mankind occurred near Jerusalem: this was the birth of Christ at Bethlehem. From that time, Bethlehem where Christ was born, Nazareth and Galilee where he lived, Jerusalem where he preached and was crucified and buried, became Christianity's holiest places.

The Jews revolted twice against the Romans, first in AD 66-70 and again in AD 132-5 (Bar-Kochba revolt). Following the first revolt, Titus destroyed the city and the Temple. After its destruction in AD 70, Jerusalem 'never again revived as a Jewish city'.[18] After the second revolt, the Jews were either killed or sold into slavery and dispersed to the far corners of the Roman Empire. When the new city of Jerusalem was rebuilt after AD 135 by the Roman Emperor Hadrian, it was given the name of Aelia Capitolina and a decree was issued which prohibited under penalty of death the presence of Jews in the city. The prohibition on the presence of Jews in Jerusalem was lifted after the Moslem Arab conquest. As from Hadrian's time until the reign of Constantine in the fourth century, the population of Jerusalem consisted only of Christians and pagans, the latter worshipping Roman deities and idols. As from the reign of Constantine no pagans were left in Jerusalem.

Christian Rule (323-614, 628-38, 1099-1187 and 1229-39)

After the quelling of the second Jewish revolt and the deportation of the Jews from Jerusalem, complete peace prevailed in the city for almost five centuries. During this period, namely in AD 324, occurred the transition from Roman to Byzantine rule. In AD 312 the Emperor Constantine was converted to Christianity and in AD 323 Christianity became the religion of the Byzantine Empire.

Constantine, as Emperor of the Byzantine Empire, took a special interest in Jerusalem, a city which 'by the death of the Lord Jesus

Christ had become the metropolis of Christianity'.[19] He ordered the erection of two magnificent churches in Jerusalem, the Church of the Holy Sepulchre (also called the Church of the Resurrection) and the Church of the Golgotha, both of which were completed and consecrated in AD 336. His mother Empress Helena discovered what was thereafter held to be the True Cross[20] and built the Church of the Nativity in Bethlehem — which still exists today — and the Church of the Ascension on the Mount of Olives. Under Christian rule Jerusalem began to attract Christian pilgrims and Palestine as a whole became a centre of eremitic life. Men flocked from all quarters to live as hermits in the Holy Land, and the country was soon dotted with a number of monasteries.

Under Byzantine rule Jerusalem prospered as a commercial centre and became one of the richest in the East. The Persians cast covetous eyes on it and in 614 Chosroes II, King of Persia, overran Syria and sent an army to pillage Jerusalem. In its advance on Jerusalem, the Persian army was joined by a number of Jews who were then to be found in the north of Palestine, mainly in Tiberias, Galilee and around Nazareth and 'who were determined to avail themselves of this opportunity of regaining what they considered to be their own city, and of revenging themselves upon the Christians who had excluded them from it for so many years'.[21] When the Persians captured Jerusalem, its inhabitants were massacred and a number of churches, including the Churches of the Golgotha and the Holy Sepulchre, were destroyed and the True Cross taken away by the invaders.

In 627 Heraclius, Emperor of Byzantium, invaded Persia, defeated Chosroes II, recovered the True Cross and recaptured Jerusalem where he restored the decrees of Hadrian and Constantine which forbade the Jews to enter Jerusalem.[22] The return of Jerusalem under Christian rule was, however, of short duration because ten years later the city was captured by the Moslem Arabs.

However, the Christians were destined to return to Jerusalem five centuries later. The reasons for their return were the attacks on pilgrims, the persecution of the Christian inhabitants and the jeopardy to Christian Holy Places in Jerusalem. Although Christians and Moslems lived on good terms after the Moslem Arab occupation, and Caliph Harun Al Rashid even exchanged ambassadors in 797 with Emperor Charlemagne and allowed him to restore the Church of the Holy Sepulchre, it fell to Hakem Bi Amr Illah, one of the Fatimid Caliphs, to spoil this good relationship. This ruler, who is considered by Moslem historians to have been mentally deranged, persecuted the Christians and destroyed Christian churches, including the Church of the Holy Sepulchre, which was razed to the ground in 1009. However, in 1032 it was restored. Then when in 1072 the Seljuk Turks seized Jerusalem, the position of the Christians worsened considerably and a number of them were massacred. These excesses were the main cause for the preaching of the First Crusade by Pope Urban II. The object of the Crusaders was to drive the Turks out of Jerusalem. In fact, however, the Arabs drove the Seljuk Turks out of the city and even out of Palestine before the Crusaders arrived, but this circumstance failed to halt their invasion.

In 1099 the Crusaders captured Jerusalem and established there the Latin Kingdom of Jerusalem. This kingdom, whose first ruler was Godefroi de Bouillon, was run on the European feudal system and extended from Aqaba to Beirut and from the Mediterranean to the Jordan River. Its rule in Jerusalem lasted eighty-eight years until 1187 when the city was reconquered by Saladin (Salah-Id-Din Ayoubi).[23] However, in 1229 Jerusalem again returned for a short time to Christian hands, as a result of a temporary cession by its Moslem ruler to the German Emperor, Frederick II, who had undertaken a crusade for its liberation. But the city was retaken by the Moslem Arabs ten years later.

In all, Christian rule in Jerusalem, Byzantine and Crusader, lasted four centuries.

Moslem Rule (Arab and Turkish) (638-1099, 1187-1229 and 1239-1917)

In 638 the Moslem Arabs[24] who had fanned out from the Arabian Peninsula reached Jerusalem and laid siege to it. After four months, the inhabitants sued for peace, but insisted that the Caliph Omar Ibn Al Khattab should come in person to accept the surrender of the city. And thus Omar, the second Caliph, came to Jerusalem and Sophronius, its Orthodox Patriarch, surrendered to him the city after having obtained from him a formal written pledge for the respect of the Christian churches and the security of its inhabitants.

Arab historians record with detail Omar's entry into Jerusalem after its surrender. Escorted by the Patriarch Sophronius he visited the site of the Temple and the Church of the Holy Sepulchre. While he was in the Church of the Holy Sepulchre the time for prayer came. Omar, it is said, was invited by the Patriarch to pray in the Church, but he refused for fear, he told the prelate, that the Moslems might appropriate it at a later time on the ground that he had prayed there. So he went out and prayed at a spot facing the Holy Sepulchre and on this spot a mosque was erected which exists today and is called the Omari Mosque.

Another picturesque detail given by historians concerns the extreme simplicity of Caliph Omar's dress and appearance on this historic occasion. In contrast with the extravagant pomp of the Byzantine rulers and clergy and the luxurious and gilded vestments which they wore on ceremonial occasions, the successor of the Prophet of Islam entered the city on his camel, clad in a mantle of camel hair.

Omar ordered the erection of a mosque on the site of the rock which, in accordance with Islamic tradition, bears a mark of the footprint of the Prophet when he ascended to heaven during his Night Journey. This mosque which originally was a modest construction was replaced by the famous mosque built by Caliph Abdul Malek in 691 and became known as the Mosque of the Dome of the Rock. Some wrongly call it the Mosque of Omar despite the fact that Caliph Omar had no part in its building. Later, another famous mosque, called the Mosque of Al-Aqsa, was built by the Omayyads close by between 705 and 714. Since then these two mosques and their enclosure called *Haram Al-Sharif* (which means Noble Shrine) have come to be considered as the most sacred sanctuaries of Islam in Jerusalem.

From 638 until 1517 Jerusalem was ruled by the Arab Caliphs — Omayyads, Abbassids, Fatimids and their successors — except for a short period between 1072 and 1092 when the Seljuk Turks seized the city and the two periods of Crusader domination mentioned above between 1099-1187 and 1229-39. In all, Arab rule until the Turkish occupation lasted almost eight centuries.

In 1517 the Ottoman Turks under Sultan Selim captured Jerusalem. The transition from Arab to Turkish rule entailed no demographic or other change in the city, except a change of administration. The Turks did not colonize Jerusalem or any part of Palestine. A very small number of Turks held key posts in the administration, but the large majority of officials as well as the population remained basically Arab. Turkish rule continued until the twentieth century except for a short interlude of ten years (1831-41) during which Mohamed Ali, the Turkish Governor of Egypt, proclaimed Egypt's independence and seized Jerusalem and the rest of Palestine.

During Turkish times the question of the Holy Places, in Jerusalem and Bethlehem in particular, engaged the attention of the authorities by reason of the continuous quarrels between the Christian communities — principally Latin, Orthodox and Armenian — over their respective rights. The Turkish Government settled the recurring disputes by legislation and in 1757 and 1852 it issued *firmans*, or imperial decrees, which defined the rights of the respective communities to Christian sanctuaries in Jerusalem and Bethlehem. The rules so laid down came to be known as the *status quo*.

The question of the Holy Places and the rights of the Christians in Palestine were not confined to the local sphere but assumed international importance in the Capitulations. These were treaties which were made between the Sultan of Turkey and European powers. The first Capitulations were concluded in 1535 between François I, King of France, and Suleiman the Magnificent, Sultan of Turkey, and dealt with commerce, religious freedom and consular jurisdiction. These Capitulations were renewed in 1673 and 1740 and were extended to cover political and religious privileges. Similar Capitulations were concluded between Turkey and almost all European powers.

In 1774 Russia obtained from Turkey the same rights and privileges that Turkey had accorded to France and England under the Capitulations. Thereafter, Russia claimed to be the protector of the Orthodox in Turkey in the same manner as France had become the protector of the Latins. In 1847 a small incident relating to the disappearance of the silver star which indicates the birthplace of Christ at the Church of the Nativity in Bethlehem led to a dispute between the Orthodox and Latin clergy. The dispute was espoused by their respective protectors with France backing the Latin clergy and Russia backing the Orthodox clergy. The dispute was further aggravated by a Russian demand for Turkish recognition of its right to protect all the Orthodox in Turkey. Following Turkey's refusal of the Russian demand, the Crimean War (1854-6) broke out between Russia, on the one hand, and Turkey, France and England, on the other.[25]

Turkish rule in Jerusalem ended during the First World War. Turkey's entry into the war in 1914 on the side of Germany led to much scheming over Palestine by the Allied Powers.

On the one hand, the British Government and its Allies gave the Arabs several pledges for the recognition of the independence of the Arab territories, including Palestine.[26] Concurrently with the giving of these pledges, Great Britain and France concluded on 16 May 1916 a secret accord, called the Sykes-Picot Agreement, which envisaged, amongst other things, that Palestine would be severed from Turkey and would be subjected to an international administration the form of which would be decided after consultation with Russia, the other Allies and the Sharif of Mecca.

On the other hand, in an effort to win Jewish support, the British Government promised to aid Zionist ambitions in Palestine. To that end, it issued on 2 November 1917 a statement which became known as the Balfour Declaration. In its statement the British Government declared its 'sympathy with Jewish Zionist aspirations' and viewed with favour the establishment in Palestine of a 'national home' for the Jewish people, it being clearly understood that nothing should be done which might prejudice the civil and religious rights of 'existing non-Jewish communities in Palestine', or the rights and political status enjoyed by Jews in any other country.

The Balfour Declaration, which has been described as a document in which 'one nation solemnly promised to a second nation the country of a third',[27] was rejected by the so-called 'non-Jewish communities in Palestine', that is, the Arabs of Palestine who had inhabited the country from time immemorial and whose number exceeded 90 per cent of the population.

Five weeks after the issue of the Balfour Declaration, i.e. on 9 December 1917, Jerusalem was captured by General Allenby for the Allied Powers. Turkish rule in the city had lasted exactly four centuries while Moslem rule, Arab and Turkish, lasted almost twelve centuries.

Notes

1. John Gray, *A History of Jerusalem* (Praeger, New York, 1969), p. 65.
2. Josephus Flavius, *The Great Roman-Jewish War AD66-70* (Gloucester, Mass., 1970), p. 250 (vi. 10).
3. *Jewish Encyclopedia*, Vol. VII, p. 120.
4. R. de Vaux, *Histoire Ancienne d'Israël* (Gabalda, Paris, 1971), p. 72.
5. *Encyclopaedia Britannica*, p. 1007.
6. Kathleen M. Kenyon, *Digging up Jerusalem* (Ernest Benn, London, 1974), p. 79.
7. Translation from A. Lods, *Israël* (Albin Michel, Paris, 1930), p. 419.
8. de Vaux, *Histoire Ancienne d'Israël*, p. 141.
9. See Moshe Menuhin, *The Decadence of Judaism in our Times* (Exposition Press, New York, 1965), p. 18; Walid Khalidi, *From Haven to Conquest* (Institute for Palestine Studies, Beirut, 1971), p. 18; Henry Cattan, *Palestine, The Arabs and Israel* (Longman, London, 1969), p. 6.
10. F.F. Bruce, *Israel and The Nations* (Paternoster Press, Exeter, 1963), p. 19.
11. Gray, *History of Jerusalem*, p. 75.
12. Kathleen M. Kenyon, *Archaeology of the Holy Land* (Praeger, New York, 1960), p. 240.
13. Bruce, *Israel and The Nations*, p. 30.
14. Michel Join-Lambert, *Jerusalem* (Elek Books, London, 1958), p. 55.
15. Henrich Graetz, *History of the Jews*, Vol. I (Philadelphia, 1956), p. 114.
16. Albert M. Hyamson, *Palestine Old and New* (Methuen, London, 1928), p. 76.

17. A.S. Rappoport, *Histoire de la Palestine* (Payot, Paris, 1932), p. 121.

18. Hyamson, *Palestine Old and New*, p. 83.

19. Gray, *History of Jerusalem*, p. 194.

20. During her pilgrimage to Jerusalem, Empress Helena entertained the ambition of discovering the True Cross and to this end she arranged for excavations to be made at the site of the Calvary. Three crosses were dug out but the problem remained of finding which of them was the true one. This was resolved by passing the three crosses over the face of a dying woman. It is said that the True Cross was identified when its shadow saved the dying woman. Thereupon, the True Cross was divided into two parts: one part was sent to Emperor Constantine, and the other part was deposited at the Church of the Resurrection (Rappoport, *Histoire de la Palestine*, p. 160).

21. C.M. Watson, *The Story of Jerusalem* (Dent, London, 1912), p. 128.

22. Rappoport, *Histoire de la Palestine*, p. 170.

23. Although the rule of the Latin Kingdom ended in Jerusalem in 1187, the Latin Kingdom survived with its capital at Acre until 1291.

24. It seems necessary to explain the difference between 'Arabs', 'Moslem Arabs' and 'Christian Arabs'. The Arabs were a pre-Islamic people who lived in various parts of the Middle East, including Palestine, before the advent of Christianity or Islam. Many of them were converted from paganism to Christianity, and after the Moslem conquest, many were converted to Islam. But not all the Arabs were converted to Islam, in particular the Christian Arabs who retained their religion after the Moslem conquest. It is a gross error, therefore, to imagine that the Palestine Arabs first came to the country at the time of the Moslem conquest in the seventh century for they and their ancestors lived in the country since time immemorial.

25. As to the subsequent history of the Capitulations, Turkey sought without success to abolish them at the outbreak of the First World War. However, the Capitulations were suspended by the mandate granted to Great Britain in 1922. Article 8 of the mandate provided that the privileges and immunities of foreigners, including the benefits of consular jurisdiction and protection enjoyed by Capitulation or usage in the Ottoman Empire, shall not be applicable to Palestine, but unless previously renounced, shall be re-established at the expiration of the mandate. The resolution adopted by the General Assembly on 29 November 1947, which called for the termination of the mandate and the partition of Palestine, provided that states whose nationals have enjoyed in the past privileges and immunities by Capitulation or usage in the Ottoman Empire are invited to renounce any right to their re-establishment in the proposed Arab and Jewish States and the City of Jerusalem.

26. For these pledges, see George Antonius, *The Arab Awakening* (Khayat, Beirut, 1928), and Cattan, *Palestine*, p. 9.

27. Arthur Koestler, *Promise and Fulfilment* (Macmillan, New York, 1949), p. 4.

Chapter Three

BRITISH OCCUPATION AND MANDATE, 1917-1948

Article 22 of the Covenant of the League of Nations

Consequent on the British occupation of Jerusalem in 1917, the city, with the rest of Palestine, was separated *de facto* from Turkey and came under British administration. Then on 24 July 1922 the British Government was granted by the Council of the League of Nations a mandate to administer the country under Article 22 of the Covenant of the League which was adopted by the Paris Peace Conference in 1919 and was incorporated in the Treaty of Versailles.

In application of the principle of the rejection of annexation of conquered territory adopted by the Allied Powers, Article 22 of the Covenant of the League of Nations laid down the concept of mandates for the Arab territories detached from Turkey. The first paragraph of Article 22 stated:

> To those colonies and territories which as a consequence of the late war have ceased to be under the sovereignty of the states which formerly governed them and which are inhabited by peoples not yet able to stand by themselves under the strenuous conditions of the modern world, there should be applied the principle that the well-being and development of such peoples form a sacred trust of civilization and that securities for the performance of this trust should be embodied in this Covenant.

The fourth paragraph of Article 22 further provided:

> Certain communities formerly belonging to the Turkish Empire have reached a stage of development where their existence as independent nations can be provisionally recognized, subject to the rendering of administrative advice and assistance by a Mandatory until such time as they are able to stand alone. The wishes of these communities must be a principal consideration in the selection of the Mandatory.

In execution of this provision five new states were created in the Middle East. These were: Iraq, Lebanon, Palestine, Syria and Transjordan (which subsequently altered its name to the Hashemite Kingdom of Jordan). It was the intention to subject these states to mandates but Iraq resisted the imposition of a mandate and proclaimed its independence. Syria and Lebanon were subjected to a French mandate while Palestine and Transjordan were subjected to a British mandate.

As a result of these political developments that resulted in Palestine becoming a separate and independent state, though subject to a temporary mandate, Jerusalem, its principal and historic city, became the capital of the new state.

Mandate over Palestine

The mandate granted to the British Government over Palestine was purportedly made under Article 22 of the Covenant of the League of Nations. In fact, however, its terms were settled behind the back of the Palestinians by the British Government 'in consultation with Zionist representatives'[1] and it constituted an abuse and a distortion of Article 22 in two respects.

First, instead of implementing the original and basic objective of Article 22 to develop self-government and help Palestine stand on its own feet as a fully independent state, the mandate added a second objective which required the Mandatory to put into effect the declaration made by the British Government on 2 November 1917 (Balfour Declaration) to place the country under such political, administrative and economic conditions as would secure the establishment of the Jewish national home. To effectuate this objective, the Administration of Palestine was required to facilitate Jewish immigration.

Secondly, the mandate further deviated from Article 22 which had envisaged that the rôle of the Mandatory would be restricted to rendering 'administrative advice and assistance' by giving to the Mandatory instead 'full powers of legislation and administration'. Obviously, the Mandatory needed such full powers of legislation and administration to impose on the Palestinians by force of arms the implementation of the Balfour Declaration and Jewish immigration into their country.

The Palestinians rejected the mandate and never conceded its validity just as they had rejected the Balfour Declaration and never accepted its validity. In fact, the history of the mandate is the history of the struggle of the Palestinians against the Balfour Declaration, Jewish immigration and the establishment of a Jewish national home in Palestine.

Armed with the mandate, using the might of the British Empire and seconded by the forces of Zionism, the British Government, neglecting the basic objective of, and justification for, the mandate,[2] concentrated upon implementing the Balfour Declaration and facilitating large-scale Jewish immigration against the will and over the opposition of the people of Palestine.

Jewish Immigration

The Jewish immigration permitted by the British Government during the mandate materially affected the demographic situation in Palestine and the character of Jerusalem. The Jewish population of Palestine increased more than tenfold. From 56,000 in 1918, the number of Jews rose to 608,230 in 1946, while the Arab population merely doubled as a result of natural increase, rising during the same period from 650,000 to 1,348,000. As to the Jewish population of Jerusalem, it tripled during the same period, rising from 33,971 to 99,400.

The opposition of the Palestinians to this Jewish immigration was expressed by riots, demonstrations and disturbances in 1920, 1921, 1929 and a rebellion which broke out in 1936 and lasted three years.

Jerusalem was the scene of many of these riots. The disturbances of 1929 erupted in Jerusalem and were sparked off by a provocative march of Jewish youths to the Wailing Wall during which they unveiled the Zionist flag and sang the Zionist national anthem. This act, added to the existing tension over Jewish immigration, was construed by the Moslems as endangering their Holy Places in Jerusalem and led to a bloody conflict which took hundreds of lives on both sides.

The Wailing Wall

Following the bloody disturbances of 1929 and in view of Jewish claims in respect of the Wailing Wall, the British Government proposed to the Permanent Mandates Commission of the League of Nations (which supervised the mandatory administration over Palestine) the appointment of a Commission to examine the question of Jewish and Moslem rights and claims relating to the Wailing Wall. An International Commission was appointed in May 1930 to determine such rights and claims. In its report, published in December 1930, the Commission ruled that Moslems possessed the sole proprietary rights to the Wailing

Wall and adjoining pavement which formed part of the *Haram Al-Sharif*, but that the Jews possessed the right of free access to it for the purpose of devotions. It should be emphasized, however, that at no time did the dispute in 1929 regarding the Wailing Wall involve any denial by the Moslems of the right of the Jews to pray at the Wailing Wall. The dispute arose from 'innovations' which the Jews sought to introduce, such as the bringing of chairs and screens to the site, which practice, it was feared, could, if it were allowed, evolve into a claim of ownership.

The Peel Commission

After the outbreak of the rebellion in 1936, the British Government appointed a Royal Commission to inquire into the situation and recommend a solution. This Royal Commission, which came to be known as the Peel Commission, investigated the unrest and found that its causes lay in the opposition of the Arabs to Jewish immigration, their desire for national independence and their fear of the establishment of the Jewish national home. The Commission recommended the partition of Palestine into Arab and Jewish States and the establishment of a permanent mandate to be exercised by the British Government over Jerusalem, Bethlehem, Nazareth and Lake Tiberias (Cmd. 5479). The Royal Commission justified its proposal for a separate régime for Jerusalem and Bethlehem by the following consideration:

> The partition of Palestine is subject to the overriding necessity of keeping the sanctity of Jerusalem and Bethlehem inviolate. That, in the fullest sense of the mandatory phrase is 'a sacred trust of civilization' — a trust on behalf not merely of the peoples of Palestine but of multitudes in other lands to whom these places, one or both, are Holy Places.

The Arabs rejected the partition plan proposed by the Royal Commission. As to the Jews, they suggested a different partition plan, and further proposed the partition of the city of Jerusalem between the Jewish State and the British Government as a mandatory power.

However, on further investigation by another Royal Commission, called the Woodhead Commission, which was set up in 1938, the partition of Palestine was found impracticable (Cmd. 5854) and was abandoned.

Jewish Terrorism

In 1939, the British Government realized that continued Jewish immigration into Palestine caused serious prejudice to the Palestinian Arabs and that it was its duty under the mandate to safeguard their rights. The British Government also realized, somewhat belatedly, that the purpose of the mandate was to lead Palestine to independence. Consequently, it issued on 17 May 1939 a White Paper (Cmd. 6018) in which it declared its intention to limit Jewish immigration to 75,000 persons over the next five years and to grant to Palestine its independence after ten years. After the period of five years no further Jewish immigration would be allowed except with Arab consent.

The Zionist Jews fought this White Paper by a campaign of violence and terrorism. Three Jewish para-military organizations, the Haganah, the Irgun Zvai Leumi and the Stern Gang, joined forces to perpetrate a series of terrorist attacks against British officials in Palestine with the avowed objective of forcing the British Government to withdraw the limitation which it had set upon Jewish immigration. To this end, the Jews dynamited government offices, sabotaged public installations, killed, abducted and flogged British soldiers and government officials.[3]

One particularly heinous outrage was the blowing up by the Irgun on 22 July 1946 of the headquarters of the Palestine Government at the King David Hotel in Jerusalem. The terrorists deposited explosives in the basement of the hotel and blew up the entire southern half of the east wing, causing the death of 91 persons and the wounding of 45 others. Menachem Begin, who subsequently became Israel's Prime Minister, was at the time the leader of the Irgun.

Partition of Palestine and Internationalization of Jerusalem

In 1947 the situation of the British Government became impossible. Unable in conscience to permit any further Jewish immigration into Palestine against the will of the majority of its inhabitants, plagued by Zionist demands to admit more and more immigrants, subjected to strong pressure by the US Government to increase Jewish immigration into Palestine despite the fact that it had itself closed its own doors to Jewish immigrants, and harassed by Zionist terrorist outrages, the British Government decided to refer to the UN the question of the future government of Palestine.

This question was considered at a special session of the General

Assembly held in April and May 1947. On 15 May the General Assembly appointed the UN Special Commission on Palestine (UNSCOP) to study the problem and to submit such proposals as it might consider appropriate for its solution.

The Palestinians unwisely boycotted UNSCOP, a fact which did not prevent it from submitting its report to the General Assembly in September 1947. Two plans for the solution of the Palestine problem, a majority plan and a minority plan, were offered in the report.

The majority plan proposed the termination of the mandate, the partition of Palestine into Arab and Jewish States and the establishment of the City of Jerusalem and its environs as a *corpus separatum* which would be placed under a special international régime to be administered by the Trusteeship Council on behalf of the UN.

The minority plan also recommended the termination of the mandate but proposed the establishment of a federal state consisting of Arab and Jewish States with Jerusalem as the capital.

The Palestinians and the Arab States opposed the partition of Palestine and the creation of a Jewish State. They also rejected the internationalization of Jerusalem. As to the Jews, they pretended to accept partition, with reluctance. Despite Arab opposition, the General Assembly, some of whose members were pressured by the US Government[4] and the Zionists, adopted on 29 November 1947, by a vote of 33 to 13 with 10 abstentions, resolution 181 (II) for the partition of Palestine and the internationalization of Jerusalem, basically on the lines suggested by the majority report. The resolution also made provision for the appointment of a Commission, named the Palestine Commission, to be charged with the provisional administration of Palestine on the withdrawal of the Mandatory and with putting into effect the partition plan and the international régime of Jerusalem.

Chaos and War

The Palestine Commission was unable to assume its administrative functions owing to the opposition of the British Government as Mandatory, which would not allow a parallel authority in Palestine before its withdrawal. This was the ostensible reason but, in fact, the British Government was not satisfied with the justice of the partition plan and did not wish to participate in its implementation. Neither could the Palestine Commission assume its functions after the termination of the mandate by reason of the complete chaos which then prevailed. All that the

Commission did was to report on the collapse of law and order and the need for an international police force.

World opinion was very much disturbed over the disorders which broke out in Palestine and, in particular, in Jerusalem following the UN resolution for partition of the country. This led to a spate of UN resolutions which did not prevent the situation from deteriorating. The most important of those resolutions were the following:

Resolution 44 adopted by the Security Council on 1 April 1948 at the request of the US Government to convene a special session of the General Assembly to consider further the question of the government of Palestine. At this special session, the US advocated a suspension of action on the partition plan and a temporary trusteeship over Palestine. This proposal, however, was vigorously opposed by the Jews and eventually was not endorsed.

Resolution 48 adopted by the Security Council on 23 April 1948 which established a Truce Commission for Palestine composed of representatives of the members of the Security Council which had consular officers in Jerusalem. The Truce Commission was composed of the American, Belgian and French consuls at Jerusalem.

Resolution 187 adopted by the General Assembly on 6 May 1948 which recommended the appointment of a Special Municipal Commissioner for the administration of Jerusalem who, although appointed, was unable to assume his functions.

Despite all these resolutions the UN was unable to redress the situation or to prevent it from drifting from bad to worse. Even the Mandatory abandoned all efforts to maintain law and order and began to withdraw its forces from Palestine. The partition resolution had envisaged that the mandate should end as soon as possible but not later than 1 August 1948, but the Mandatory advanced the date to 15 May. In fact, the British Government withdrew its forces one day earlier, that is on 14 May, and left Palestine hurriedly without even making any arrangements for any successor administration and without handing over power to any organized authorities.

On the same day as the British withdrawal, the Jews proclaimed the State of Israel purportedly under the UN partition resolution. But the state which emerged was at complete variance organically, territorially and demographically with the Jewish State envisaged by the resolution.

Thereupon complete chaos prevailed in the whole of Palestine and a war broke out on 15 May between the neighbouring Arab States and the new State of Israel. Jerusalem became a battlefield, as we shall see in the next chapter.

As to the UN, which by its resolution for the partition of Palestine and the creation of a Jewish State had let loose forces which it was unable to control or contain, it washed its hands of the mess it had helped to create by adopting on 14 May a resolution for the appointment of a Mediator to use his good offices to assure the safety of the population of Palestine and the protection of the Holy Places and to promote a peaceful adjustment of the future situation of Palestine. Count Folke Bernadotte of Sweden was appointed as the Mediator to perform these miracles.

Notes

1. H.W.V. Temperley, *History of the Peace Conference of Paris*, Vol. VI (Hodder and Stoughton, London, 1924), p. 174.
2. On two occasions, in 1922 and in 1935, the Mandatory made proposals for the establishment of a Legislative Council, but on both occasions the proposals were thwarted by the Jews who did not want self-government for Palestine so long as they were a minority. These proposals were also criticized by the Palestinians for not giving due consideration to their majority status.
3. For details about Jewish acts of violence, see Government of Palestine, *A Survey of Palestine*, Vol. I, pp. 56-7; the British Statement on Acts of Violence, Cmd. 6873 (1946); S.N. Fisher, *The Middle East* (Routledge and Kegan Paul, London, 1959), p. 579; G. Kirk, *The Middle East 1945-1950* (Oxford University Press, London, 1954), pp. 209-13 and 218-23.
4. Regarding the pressures brought to bear by the US Government, and in particular, by President Truman, on UN members to vote in favour of partition, see Henry Cattan, *Palestine and International Law*, 2nd edn (Longman, London, 1976), pp. 82-7.

Chapter Four

THE BATTLE FOR JERUSALEM, 1948

Displacement of the Arabs

The battle for Jerusalem did not break out on the termination of the mandate: it erupted before.

Judging Jewish intentions on the basis of the actual events that occurred, it would seem that the Jews had two objectives in the battle for Jerusalem.

The first was to displace the Palestinians from the city. This objective was not limited to Jerusalem only, but extended to every village, city or territory which they occupied or planned to occupy and make part of the Jewish State. The Zionist Jewish ambition was to establish a state that would be racially, religiously and exclusively Jewish. This notion echoed some of the attitudes of Biblical times. Referring to the Jews who had returned from the exile at Babylon, Kathleen Kenyon states:

> At this stage, the Biblical record (Ezra 4:1-3) brings into prominence the sense of the returned exiles. They believed that they alone had maintained unsullied the true religion of Yahweh. They refused to allow the inhabitants of the old northern kingdom of Israel, racially contaminated by the immigrants transplanted after the Assyrian absorption of Israel at the end of the eighth century B.C., to have any share in the rebuilding of the Temple.[1]

In the Zionist creed, the exclusivist Jewishness of the state which they planned to establish would require the displacement of the original inhabitants from the land.

To achieve their objective, the Jews resorted to terrorism against the Palestinian Arabs with the purpose of causing their flight from their homes. Unfortunately, they succeeded in achieving their purpose. At the end of 1947 and during the remaining months of the mandate, they turned against the Palestinian Arabs the terrorist machine which they had perfected in their campaign of violence against the British. The chronology of events during this period makes sad reading and sheds light upon the horrible acts perpetrated by Jewish terrorists in Palestine.

This does not imply that acts of violence were restricted to the Jewish side only. The Arabs also were responsible for many acts of violence against the Jews. But the acts of the two sides cannot be equated. Acts of violence on the part of the Palestinian Arabs were prompted by the will to resist the usurpation of their country by a foreign people and to prevent the establishment of an alien state on the soil of their homeland. Acts of violence by Jewish terrorists were designed to displace the original Arab population by force and fear and to establish a Jewish state which, in their view, would be racially pure.

Although Jewish terrorists struck in various parts of Palestine, their worst deeds were perpetrated in and around Jerusalem which was their prime target. Among Jewish exploits were the dynamiting of houses over the heads of their occupants,[2] the bombing of crowds in public places and the murder of innocent people.

Deir Yassin Massacre

One particular terrorist outrage must be mentioned not only by reason of its revolting nature, but also because of its disastrous effect on the Arab population and its influence on the course of events. This was the massacre by troops of the Irgun Zvai Leumi on 9 April 1948 of the inhabitants of Deir Yassin, a small peaceful village which lies one and a half miles to the west of Jerusalem and is located in the *còrpus separatum*. An authentic account of this savage and cold-blooded massacre was given by Jacques de Reynier, the Chief Delegate of the International Red Cross who, at the risk of his life, was able to reach the village and witness the aftermath of the tragedy.

> Three hundred persons, were massacred . . . without any military reason or provocation of any kind, old men, women, children, newly-born, were savagely assassinated with grenades and knives by Jewish troops of the Irgun, perfectly under the control and direction of their chiefs.[3]

Moreover, to make sure that the massacre had its intended effect on the Arab population, the few survivors, including some women, were paraded by Irgun forces in three trucks in the streets of Jerusalem[4] to be shown as the prize of their 'military victory',[5] and on the same night the Jewish terrorist leaders who planned and executed the outrage held a press conference and boasted of their deed.[6]

Dr Stephen Penrose, President of the American University of Beirut, explained the connection between the Deir Yassin massacre and the exodus of the Palestinian Arabs in 1948 in these terms:

> On both sides dreadful deeds were committed, but, in the main, the Zionists made better use of terrorist tactics which they learned only too well at the hands of Nazi taskmasters. There is no question but that frightful massacres such as that which took place at Deir Yassin in April 1948 were perpetrated for the major purpose of frightening the Arab population and causing them to take flight. The Zionist radio repeated incessantly for the benefit of Arab listeners 'Remember Deir Yassin'. It is small wonder that many Arab families began a hasty exodus from the battle area and from sectors which might soon become battlegrounds. Terror is contagious, and it built up the tremendous migration which has led to the results which may be witnessed in the refugee camps.[7]

The number of Arabs who were displaced from Jerusalem by terror, hostilities or expulsion was not determined with any precision because there was no census of the refugees nor any breakdown of their number according to place of origin. However, the bulk of the refugees from Jerusalem came from the Arab quarters of modern Jerusalem which were occupied by Israeli forces and completely emptied of their inhabitants. A rough estimate of non-Jews who lived in the New City in 1945 was given by Rev. Charles T. Bridgeman in a communication to the Trusteeship Council dated 13 January 1950 as being 24,000 Christians and 21,000 Moslems (UN Doc.A/1286). These figures do not include Arab inhabitants in the Old City or in the vicinity of Jerusalem. Since almost all the inhabitants of the New City and its vicinity were forced to abandon their homes, one can estimate the number of Arab refugees in 1948 from Jerusalem and its vicinity to have been between 50,000 to 60,000. This represented almost two-thirds of the Arab population of the *corpus separatum* which was estimated by the UN in 1947 at 60,560 Moslems and 44,850 Christians (UN Doc.A/AC 14/32, p. 304).

Jewish Plan to Seize Jerusalem

The second Jewish objective was to seize Jerusalem. Taking advantage of the fact that the neighbouring Arab States could not enter Palestine while the British Government maintained its forces in the country, and taking advantage also of the fact that the Palestine Arabs had been systematically disarmed by the British Government on account of their opposition to the Balfour Declaration and to Jewish immigration, the Jews began to lay their plans to seize Jerusalem long before the mandate came to an end. John Bagot Glubb who commanded in 1948 the Arab Legion of Jordan puts it on record that the command of the Irgun had defined Jerusalem as one of its objectives several months before the end of the mandate.[8]

The Jews had at first accepted, or feigned to accept, the partition resolution, including its provision for the internationalization of Jerusalem, because it offered a basis for the establishment of a Jewish state. But they wanted a much bigger slice of the territory of Palestine than the mere 57 per cent of its area which was allotted to them by the partition plan. Above all, they wanted Jerusalem which had been the subject of their dreams and aspirations during many centuries. So they decided that in any event they would establish a Jewish State, regardless of the conditions and boundaries laid down by the partition resolution, and at the expense of the areas reserved for the Arab State and for the *corpus separatum* of Jerusalem. These considerations explain why the proclamation of the Jewish State made on 14 May 1948 kept silent upon the question of its boundaries. That such silence was not an oversight but quite deliberate has since been admitted by the framers of the proclamation.

The plan to seize Jerusalem was put into effect before the withdrawal of the Mandatory. In fact, all the western part of the *corpus separatum* and some parts of the modern section of Jerusalem were seized by Jewish forces when British forces and the British High Commissioner were still present in Jerusalem. Two Arab residential quarters of modern Jerusalem, namely Katamon and Sheikh Jarrah, were seized and occupied by Jewish forces on 25 and 30 April respectively. Other Arab quarters of modern Jerusalem were overrun by Jewish forces on 14 and 15 May. Thus the Jews had completed the occupation of most of modern Jerusalem before the day on which war broke out between Israel and the Arab States.

Mr Pablo de Azcarate, Secretary of the Consular Truce Commission, has described events at Jerusalem on 14 May. The British High Commissioner left Jerusalem on the morning of that day by air for Haifa whence he sailed home. He was followed by British troops so that at about two o'clock in the afternoon not a single British soldier remained in Jerusalem. Here are the events that followed:

Hardly had the last English soldier disappeared than the Jews launched their offensive, consolidating their possession of Katamon which they occupied two weeks before and seizing the German Colony and the other southern districts of Jerusalem. The last remaining Arabs were liquidated, and from henceforth, the Jews were absolute masters of the southern part of the city.[9]

Pablo de Azcarate then described the efforts that were made by the Commission on the afternoon of 14 May to secure a suspension of hostilities. It was not possible, he observed, to arrange a meeting between the parties because the Arab representatives who were in the Old City could not cross over to the French Consulate which was in the New City to attend the meeting with the Commission. They claimed that the Jews, in spite of their promises of safe conduct, did not cease firing so as to permit their passage. Pablo de Azcarate makes the following comment:

The Jews, already perfectly organized, were carrying out methodically their plan to seize the whole of modern Jerusalem and were naturally very far from thinking of suspending, far less abandoning, the execution of this plan in deference to our telephone calls; and I do not think it would be very wide of the mark to say that with their passive resistance to a cease-fire in the zone which the Arab delegates would have to cross in order to reach the French Consulate, they rendered all negotiations impossible without incurring the responsibility for a blank refusal. As for the Arabs, it is not easy to say what their real attitude was, for the simple reason that probably they themselves would not have been able to say what it was. The so-called Arab forces were 'irregulars', indifferently controlled by improvised leaders under the nominal authority of the Arab Higher Committee. Possibly, at that moment they would have been glad of a suspension of hostilities and their explanation that the Jewish forces, by their fire, were preventing their delegates from reaching the French Consulate was sincere. Should this be so, one can but pay a tribute of admiration to the ingenuity of the Jewish leaders who appeared to be giving the greatest facilities for a settlement in which they were not interested and which they themselves rendered impossible.[10]

The Arab quarters of modern Jerusalem were completely undefended and their inhabitants had either fled or were killed. In those quarters where the Jews encountered resistance, such as in Musrarah, the Arab residents were terrorized by the Haganah which had been proclaimed the official army of the new State of Israel. The Arab residents were ordered under dire threats to leave the city. Watching from the Italian Hospital the fighting which was going on in the vicinity on 15 May, Harry Levin, a Jewish newspaper correspondent, says:

> Nearby, a loudspeaker burst out in Arabic: 'Haganah broadcasting to civilian Arabs, urging them to leave the district before 5.15 a.m. Take pity on your wives and children and get out of this blood bath', it said. 'Surrender to us with your arms. No harm will come to you. Or get out by the Jericho road, that is still open to you. If you stay, you invite disaster.'[11]

The Arab quarters of modern Jerusalem which were seized were residential areas and constituted the most beautiful parts of the city. Hence, it is an error to imagine that in 1948 the Israelis seized the Jewish section of the city, and the Arabs seized the Arab part. In fact, the larger part of the modern section was inhabited by two-thirds of the Arab population of Jerusalem and was largely Arab-owned.

Looting

One of the first acts of the Jewish forces at the time of their capture of the Arab quarters in modern Jerusalem was to loot the Arab dwellings which, in most cases, were left intact with their contents by reason of the precipitate flight or liquidation of their owners.[12] This was a massive plunder reminiscent of uncivilized times. George Kirk wrote:

> It was apparently at Jaffa that Jewish troops first succumbed to the temptation to indulge in wholesale looting . . . and within a few days Jewish troops were looting the newly captured Arab suburbs of Jerusalem (see Kimche, *Seven Fallen Pillars*, p. 224; Levin, *Jerusalem Embattled*, pp. 116, 135-36, 226). Ben Gurion himself afterwards admitted that the extent to which responsible Jews of all classes became involved was a shameful and distressing spectacle (*Israel Government Handbook*, 5712, London, Seymour Press, 1951/52).[13]

Attacks on Old City

After the Jews overran the Arab quarters of modern Jerusalem, they 'attacked the Old City on three fronts, in a determined effort to link up with those entrenched in the Jewish quarter and to take the city by storm'.[14] Harry Levin wrote in his diary:

> Haganah is trying desperately to relieve the quarter. Today [18 May] they got right up to the walls. During the night Palmach seized Deir Abu Tor and immediately pushed across the vale of Hinnom and captured Mount Zion. Without a pause, they went for Zion Gate with bazoukas, their heaviest weapons, but failed. Another unit stormed strongpoints around Jaffa Gate, but couldn't breach the Gate itself. Last night's objective was a concerted attempt to smash through three gates: none of it was achieved.[15]

From 14 to 18 May the situation within Jerusalem was critical for the Arab defenders. However, the Jewish attacks were defeated. The credit for saving the city on this occasion must go not only to its brave Palestinian defenders, but also to Suleiman the Magnificent, the Turkish Sultan, who in 1542 built the massive walls that surround it.

During the first few days, the battle for Jerusalem was fought exclusively between Palestine Arab irregulars, on the one hand, and organized and trained Jewish military forces, on the other. The latter were composed of men who before their emigration to Palestine had seen military or war service. No military forces of any Arab State were then anywhere in or near the city. On 15 May forces of the Arab Legion of Jordan moved to Jericho, a small town which lies some twenty miles to the east of Jerusalem, but they remained stationed there and did not approach Jerusalem in which the fighting was raging. John Bagot Glubb, British Commander of the Arab Legion, explains the reason:

> Meanwhile, the Jordan Government ordered the Arab Legion not to enter Jerusalem, out of respect for the United Nations. From 15th to 19th May, the Israelis conquered most of the city, opposed only by miscellaneous parties of Arabs, defending the Arab quarters. Only on 19th May did the Arab Legion, despairing of the United Nations, enter Jerusalem and defend what it could of the Arab city.[16]

It seems necessary to stress the point that it was Israel, not Jordan, which first attacked Jerusalem in 1948 and wrecked the plan for its internationalization, because Israel has not hesitated to distort the true facts. Answering an allegation made by Israel at the UN that in 1948 Jordan had committed 'an aggressive invasion' of Jerusalem in breach of the injunctions of the Security Council, the Government of Jordan declared in a communication to the UN:

> The truth of the matter in this connexion is that the Jordan Army came into Jerusalem on 18 May 1948, that is, three days after the end of the British mandate, at the desperate insistence and appeal of the beleaguered Arab citizens, to save what was left of the whole city – only a small part of it – after they had lost their bigger part outside its walls to the Israeli gangs and forces before and after the end of the mandate. For three days and nights, between the 15th and 18th of that fateful month, the heavily armed Israeli forces mercilessly pounded the historic walled city with the determined aim of achieving its occupation. And but for the heroic resistance of the citizens, largely unarmed and with no regular forces or supplies to assist them in putting up some kind of a coherent defence, the Israeli onslaught came within a hairbreadth of achieving its aggressive goal on the midnight of 18 May 1948. Prior to that and while the British Mandatory was still responsible for law and order in the city, Jewish forces belonging to the Haganah and the Irgun and Stern gangs had already been rampaging and annexing most Arab quarters in the New City and its environs. The unspeakable massacres of hundreds of men, women and children and the dumping of their mutilated bodies in the village wells of Deir Yassin – a suburb of Jerusalem – is but one of the more notorious crimes committed against the citizens of Jerusalem and its environs.[17]

Egypt was the only other Arab State which sent armed forces in the direction of Jerusalem. Egyptian forces entered Palestine on 15 May and split into two columns: the first moved along the coast towards Gaza, the second advanced along the inland road to Beersheba, Hebron and Bethlehem. But this second column attacked only one Jewish position, the settlement of Ramat Rahel, near Bethlehem, and did not advance on Jerusalem.

With the arrival of the Arab Legion forces in Jerusalem, the fighting in the Old City was intensified and the Jewish quarter surrendered on 28 May. Some 1,200 men, women and children were released to Jewish lines in the New City and 290 Haganah soldiers were taken prisoner. After taking the Jewish quarter in the Old City, the Arab Legion made no attempt to recover the Arab quarters which had been occupied by the Jews in modern Jerusalem.

On 29 May 1948 the Security Council ordered a four-week truce. The truce was arranged by Count Folke Bernadotte, the UN Mediator, and came into force on 11 June 1948. This truce helped the Jews to improve their military position and to receive supplies so that on the resumption of the fighting they were able to seize Lydda and Ramleh and to open the road from Tel-Aviv to Jerusalem. On 15 July the Security Council ordered an unlimited ceasefire to take effect at 3.00 p.m. GMT on 18 July. It is significant to observe that on the day preceding the coming into effect of the ceasefire, i.e. on 17 July, Jewish forces launched a fierce assault on the Old City. This attack which failed took place at a time when not a single Jew was to be found in the Old City as the Jews of the Jewish quarter had already surrendered on 28 May and had been moved away. Quite obviously, the attack on this occasion did not aim at relieving the situation in the Jewish quarter but simply aimed at the capture of the Old City, an aim which they realized nineteen years later.

Arab Quarters of Modern Jerusalem

The military situation in Jerusalem remained static as established in May 1948 and was eventually frozen by the Armistice Agreement concluded between Israel and Jordan on 3 April 1949.

The Armistice Agreement left Israel in occupation of modern Jerusalem, including twelve of its fifteen Arab residential quarters, emptied of their inhabitants, and Jordan in occupation of the Old City.

The Arab quarters which Israeli forces seized in 1948 and which are still in Israeli hands are the following: Katamon, Musrarah, Talbieh, Upper Bakaa, Lower Bakaa, the Greek and German Colonies, Sheikh Jarrah, Deir Abu Tor, Mamillah, Nebi Daoud and Sheikh Bader.

Notes

1. Kathleen M. Kenyon, *Digging up Jerusalem* (Ernest Benn, London, 1974), p. 175.

2. One of the examples of this kind of terrorism was the dynamiting by the Haganah on 5 January 1948 of the Semiramis Hotel in the Arab residential quarter of Katamon in Jerusalem causing the death of twenty Arab residents and of the Spanish Consul; see *Middle East Journal* (Middle East Institute, Washington DC, 1948), p. 217.

3. Translation from Jacques de Reynier, *A Jérusalem un Drapeau Flottait sur la Ligne de Feu* (Baconnière, Neuchatel, 1950), p. 213.

4. Harry Levin, *Jerusalem Embattled* (Gollancz, London, 1950), p. 57.

5. See Menachem Begin, *The Revolt: Story of the Irgun* (Schuman, New York, 1951).

6. Edwin Samuel, *Middle East Journal*, 1949, p. 14.

7. Stephen B.L. Penrose, *The Palestine Problem: Retrospect and Prospect* (American Friends of the Middle East, New York), p. 12.

8. John Bagot Glubb, *Peace in the Holy Land* (Hodder and Stoughton, London, 1971), p. 299.

9. Pablo de Azcarate, *Mission in Palestine 1948-1952* (Middle East Institute, Washington DC, 1966), p. 43.

10. Ibid., p. 45.

11. Levin, *Jerusalem Embattled*, p. 160.

12. The author of this book was one of the numerous victims of the looting. His home in Jerusalem was looted, according to eye-witnesses, by the Haganah which took away his law library, valuables and household effects in seven truck loads.

13. George Kirk, *The Middle East 1945-1950* (Oxford University Press, London, 1954), p. 263.

14. A.L. Tibawi, *Jerusalem* (Institute for Palestine Studies, Beirut, 1969), p. 40.

15. Levin, *Jerusalem Embattled*, p. 159.

16. Glubb, *Peace in the Holy Land*, p. 302.

17. UN Docs. A/8657 and S/10517 of 21 January 1972.

Chapter Five

JERUSALEM BETWEEN 1948 AND 1967

Mediator's Efforts

Count Folke Bernadotte, UN Mediator for Palestine, attempted to promote a settlement of the Palestine question. He tackled three basic problems: territory, refugees and Jerusalem; and his efforts in this regard were recorded in his diary[1] and in his Progress Report to the General Assembly dated 16 September 1948.[2] However, he made no headway in his mission and mentioned in his diary (p. 209) the 'arrogance and hostility' of the Jewish Government towards the UN representatives. He himself was even regarded as an 'enemy'.

As regards the question of territory, he was informed by Moshe Shertok, the Israeli Foreign Minister, that the frontiers laid down in the UN resolution of 29 November 1947 could not be maintained but that 'the Israeli territory would have to be expanded' (p. 211 of the diary).

As to the Palestine refugees, his efforts to secure their repatriation failed for the reason that the Israeli Government showed 'nothing but hardness and obduracy towards those refugees' (p.209).

Regarding Jerusalem, Count Bernadotte suggested to Israel its inclusion in Arab territory, with municipal autonomy for the Jewish community and special arrangements for the protection of the Holy Places. This caused an uproar among the Jews. In its reply dated 5 July 1948, the Provisional Government of Israel objected to his 'deviations' from the General Assembly resolution of 29 November 1947, and particularly to his suggestion concerning the status of Jerusalem. However, in his Progress Report he recommended that the City of Jerusalem should be placed under effective UN control with maximum feasible local autonomy for its Arab and Jewish communities and full safeguards for the protection of the Holy Places.

Count Bernadotte never completed his mission for he was assassinated at Jerusalem on 17 September 1948 by Jewish terrorists.

Internationalization Reaffirmed

Although Jerusalem was occupied militarily by Israel and Jordan, the

General assembly adopted two resolutions which reaffirmed the establishment of an international régime for the city.

In a first resolution 194 (III) dated 11 December 1948, the General Assembly resolved that, in view of its association with three world religions, the Jerusalem area should be placed under effective UN control and that the Conciliation Commission (which was established by the resolution) should present to the following session detailed proposals for a permanent international régime for the Jerusalem area which would provide for maximum local autonomy for distinctive groups consistent with the special international status of the Jerusalem area.

The Conciliation Commission submitted, as requested, its proposals which envisaged the administration by Israel and Jordan of the areas held by them and the appointment of a UN Commissioner who would be charged with the protection of the Holy Places. These proposals, in fact, were not for a permanent international régime as requested by the General Assembly since they sought to consolidate the factual division of Jerusalem between Israel and Jordan with functions for the UN Commissioner limited only to the Holy Places. As these proposals deviated from the principle of the internationalization of Jerusalem, the General Assembly ignored them.

Then in a second resolution 303 (IV) adopted on 9 December 1949, the General Assembly restated its intention that Jerusalem should be placed under a permanent international régime which should envisage appropriate guarantees for the protection of the Holy Places, both within and outside Jerusalem. It confirmed specifically that the City of Jerusalem should be established as a *corpus separatum* under a special international régime to be administered by the UN. The resolution further requested the Trusteeship council to prepare and approve a Statute of Jerusalem on the lines of resolution 181 (II) and to proceed immediately with its implementation without allowing any actions taken by any government or governments to divert it from its course. On 4 April 1950 the Trusteeship Council approved a Statute for the City of Jerusalem and transmitted it to the General Assembly. This was followed by discussions at the Ad Hoc Committee and the General Assembly on the draft statute which led to no result. No action has since been taken by the UN to approve or to implement the draft statute prepared by the Trusteeship Council.

Israel and Jordan Reject Internationalization

Prior to the proclamation of the Jewish State, the Jews had made a pretence of accepting the internationalization of Jerusalem. But they hoped that eventually they would get rid of the international régime. The fact that Jewish acceptance of internationalization was purely tactical is explained by Walter Eytan, Director General of the Israeli Foreign Ministry:

> The spokesmen of the Palestine Arabs and of the Arab States rejected the internationalization of Jerusalem outright. Internationalization formed an integral part of the partition plan, whose general advantages, notably the establishment of an independent Jewish State, outweighed the bitter sacrifice involved in relinquishing the ancient capital of Israel. In any event, the international régime was, by recommendation of the General Assembly, to remain in force in the first instance for a period not exceeding ten years. The whole scheme was then to be subject to re-examination by the Trusteeship Council 'in the light of the experience acquired with its functioning', and the residents of Jerusalem were to be free 'to express by means of a referendum their wishes as to possible modifications of the régime of the City'. Since the population of Jerusalem in 1947 consisted of 100,000 Jews and 65,000 Arabs (of whom slightly more than half were Moslems), the Jewish Agency looked forward with confidence to the outcome of the proposed referendum.[3]

Walter Eytan's view in this regard calls for two comments.

First, the population figures he gives for the City of Jerusalem are erroneous since the UN estimate of the population of the *corpus separatum* was 105,540 Arabs as against 99,690 Jews.[4]

Second, it seems doubtful that a referendum destined to ascertain the wishes of the residents of Jerusalem as to 'possible modifications' includes the right to terminate the régime. Moreover, any such conclusion overlooks the fact that resolutions 194 (III) and 303 (IV) speak of a 'permanent' international régime.

In any event, the view expressed by Walter Eytan is of interest since it indicates the intentions which Israel harboured to get rid of the international régime.

Israel, however, did not wait so long or for a plebiscite to thwart the enforcement of the international régime of Jerusalem: it prevented its coming into effect by the occupation of modern Jerusalem before the termination of the mandate. Moreover, in statements which it made to the Palestine Conciliation Commission[5] and to the Ad Hoc Political Committee,[6] it indicated its opposition to the establishment of a *corpus separatum* in accordance with the internationalization plan. Referring to discussions held with the parties in March and April 1949, the Conciliation Commission put on record their respective attitudes as follows:

> 4. During the Commission's conversations in Beirut with the Arab Delegations, the latter showed themselves, in general, prepared to accept the principle of an international régime for the Jerusalem area, on condition that the United Nations should be in a position to offer the necessary guarantees regarding the stability and permanence of such a régime.
> 5. From the beginning, however, the Government of Israel, while recognizing that the Commission was bound by General Assembly resolution 194 (III), declared itself unable to accept the establishment of an international régime for the City of Jerusalem; it did, however, accept without reservation the international régime for, or the international control of, the Holy Places in the City.

The Holy Places in Jerusalem were at the time in the hands of Jordan.

Although the Conciliation Commission's report suggests that the Arab States were prepared to accept the principle of an international régime for the Jerusalem area, this was not the position of Jordan. On several occasions King Abdullah declared that he would not accept an international régime for Jerusalem.

Israel's Assurances to the UN Regarding Implementation of General Assembly Resolutions

It should be remarked that although Israel rejected the internationalization of Jerusalem, it did not immediately annex the modern section of the city. For this there was a good reason: it did not wish to jeopardize its pending application for admission to membership of the UN, particularly since at that time world opinion was very sensitive to the question of Jerusalem. On the contrary, Israel gave specific assurances to the UN regarding the implementation of General Assembly resolutions.

Israel's first application for admission to the UN was rejected by the

Security Council on 17 December 1948. When Israel renewed its application on 24 February 1949, it was invited by the General Assembly to clarify its attitude to the execution of the General Assembly's resolutions, in particular with respect to the international status of Jerusalem and the repatriation of the Palestine refugees. Several meetings of the Ad Hoc Political Committee were held, during which Israel's representative was questioned about Israel's intentions regarding the execution of General Assembly's resolutions 181 (II) and 194 (III).[7] Among the questions that were addressed to him was a specific inquiry as to whether Israel had made the required declaration to the UN for guaranteeing the Holy Places, human rights, fundamental freedoms and minority rights, as required by resolution 181 (II). Israel's representative replied that the State of Israel had given the required formal undertaking to accept the provisions of the resolution, and he referred to Security Council document S/757, which embodied the cablegram addressed by Israel's Foreign Minister to the Secretary-General of the UN on 15 May 1948. In this cablegram, Israel proclaimed its readiness to co-operate with the UN in the implementation of the resolution of 29 November 1947 and to sign the declaration and undertaking prescribed by the resolution concerning Holy Places, religious buildings, religious and minority rights and the placing of such matters under the guarantee of the UN.

Asked about the transfer by Israel of five ministries from Tel-Aviv to Jerusalem, a fact which had been construed as an annexation of the New City, Israel's representative pretended that this act was not intended to create a new political or juridical situation in the city, but merely to stimulate its economic recovery. Israel's representative, Abba Eban, said:

the re-establishment of institutions of health and learning, and of at least a proportion of the official business which had once been the main support of Jerusalem, had been indispensable to prevent the city from becoming impoverished and depressed. That was the sole motive for transferring to Jerusalem the personnel of non-political departments whose presence might stem the flight from Jerusalem and preserve the city's traditional primacy in the religious, educational and medical life of the country. No juridical facts whatever were created by such steps, which were dictated not by a desire to create new political facts, but to assist Jerusalem and to add economic recovery to the other aspects of its splendid recuperation.[8]

Needless to observe that the truth was entirely the opposite of what

Abba Eban said. Israel's representative was also specifically asked the question, 'whether, if Israel were admitted to membership in the UN, it would agree to co-operate subsequently with the General Assembly in settling the question of Jerusalem and the refugee problem or whether, on the contrary, it would invoke Article 2, paragraph 7, of the Charter which deals with the domestic jurisdiction of states'.[9] Israel's representative was most co-operative and reassuring. This is what he said in reply:

> The Government of Israel will co-operate with the Assembly in seeking a solution to those problems . . . I do not think that Article 2, paragraph 7, of the Charter, which relates to domestic jurisdiction, could possibly affect the Jerusalem problem, *since the legal status of Jerusalem is different from that of the territory in which Israel is sovereign.* My own feeling is that it would be a mistake for any of the Governments concerned to take refuge, with regard to the refugee problem, in their legal rights to exclude people from their territories . . .[10]

Israel's representative then added:

> Moreover, as a general theory — and as I explained yesterday — during the past year we arrived, in connexion with resolutions of the General Assembly, at the view that we must be very careful not to make an extreme application of Article 2, paragraph 7, if such an application would deprive Assembly decisions of all compelling force. The admission of Israel to the United Nations would obviously result in making applicable to it Article 10 of the Charter, and the General Assembly would then be able to make recommendations directly to the Government of Israel, which would I think, attribute to those resolutions extremely wide validity.[11]

The Cuban representative summed up the debate on Israel's admission in the following terms:

> Certain happenings which had shocked public opinion had perforce been investigated on different lines than would have been the case had Israel been a Member of the United Nations. The representative of Israel has given an assurance that, if that country were admitted as a Member, such matters as the settlement of frontiers, the internationalization of Jerusalem and the Arab refugee problem would

not be regarded as within its domestic jurisdiction and protected from intervention under the terms of Article 2, paragraph 7 [of the Charter].[12]

In its resolution of 11 May 1949 which admitted Israel to UN membership, the General Assembly took note of Israel's undertaking to honour the obligations of the UN Charter and of its 'declarations and explanations' before the Ad Hoc Committee in respect of the implementation of the General Assembly's resolutions of 29 November 1947 and 11 December 1948. Accordingly, Israel's admission to UN membership was not unqualified, but must be considered to have been conditional upon its assurances relating to the implementation of General Assembly resolutions, and in particular resolutions 181 (II) and 194 (III).

Annexation of Modern Jerusalem

Having gained admission to UN membership, Israel was not deterred by General Assembly resolutions 181 (II) and 194 (III) or its assurances concerning their implementation from completing its annexation of modern Jerusalem. The Israeli annexation of this part of the city was, so to speak, a creeping operation. At first, Israel proclaimed on 12 August 1948 that the area which it had occupied in Jerusalem was 'Israeli-occupied territory' subject to military administration. Then in February 1949, military rule was abolished and the Government declared that such area should no longer be considered as occupied territory. Thereupon several ministries were moved from Tel-Aviv to Jerusalem and in December 1949 the Government itself moved to Jerusalem leaving in Tel-Aviv three ministries, including the Ministry of Foreign Affairs. Immediately after, pressure developed to declare Jerusalem the capital of the State of Israel but the Knesset preferred to adopt a resolution on 23 January 1950 which proclaimed that Jerusalem has always been the capital of Israel. Since then Israel has treated modern Jerusalem as an integral part of its territory.

Alteration of Demographic Structure

On 15 May 1948 Israel found itself in control of the New City of Jerusalem and all its Arab quarters containing some ten thousand Arab homes — most of them fully furnished. Here then in Israeli hands was the whole of modern Jerusalem, emptied of its inhabitants. It was a simple matter to judaize the city by allowing Jewish settlers to move into the Arab homes. Of course, this required that the return of the Arab owners be barred. And their return was barred.

Count Bernadotte, as we have seen, exerted all efforts to secure the repatriation of the Palestine refugees. Israel, however, refused to allow their return. The UN Mediator rejected Israel's decision and recommended to the General Assembly that 'the right of the Arab refugees to return to their homes in Jewish-controlled territory at the earliest possible date should be affirmed by the United Nations'.[13] The General Assembly accepted Count Bernadotte's recommendation and in paragraph 11 of its resolution 194 (III) of 11 December 1948 called for their return. Paragraph 11 stated that the General Assembly

> 11. *Resolves* that the refugees wishing to return to their homes and live at peace with their neighbours should be permitted to do so at the earliest practicable date, and that compensation should be paid for the property of those choosing not to return and for loss or damage to property which, under principles of international law or in equity, should be made good by the Governments or authorities responsible.
> *Instructs* the Conciliation Commission to facilitate the repatriation, resettlement and economic and social rehabilitation of the refugees and the payment of compensation . . .

But Israel was adamant. It refused the repatriation of the refugees and the Conciliation Commission had to report its failure to convince Israel to accept the principle of the repatriation of the refugees.[14] Since then the General Assembly had adopted each year a resolution which called upon Israel to allow the Palestine refugees to return but Israel has rejected and ignored all such resolutions.

Instead of allowing the Palestine refugees to return to their homes, Israel encouraged a massive Jewish immigration. In 1950 it enacted the *Law of Return*, which granted to every Jew in the world potential citizenship and automatic nationality on arrival in Israel. Thus any Jew can emigrate to Israel and settle there whereas a Palestinian Arab cannot return to his home and country. Since 1948 more than two and a half million Jews have emigrated to Israel and were given the lands and homes of the Palestine refugees.

By these two measures, namely its refusal to allow the repatriation of the Palestine refugees and its installation of large numbers of settlers and immigrants, Israel has substantially altered the demographic composition of Jerusalem. The Jewish population of Jerusalem which stood in 1947 at 99,690 rose in 1967 to 194,000 while the Arab population declined during the same period from 105,540 to zero in modern Jerusalem and to 70,000 in the Old City and its environs.

Confiscation of Arab Refugee Property

In 1948 Israel seized and confiscated all property — lands, homes, businesses — that belonged to the Palestine refugees in modern Jerusalem. This confiscation was not restricted to the Jerusalem area, but was enforced in all the territory of Palestine that fell under Israeli control.[15] The seizure was carried out under the Absentee Property Regulations (1948) and the confiscation was consummated by the Absentee Property Law (1950). This last enactment purported to authorize the so-called Custodian of Absentee Property to sell 'absentee' property — as Arab refugee property was deceitfully described — at its 'official value'. This formula was nothing but a thin disguise for its confiscation at a nominal consideration. All the Arab residential quarters of modern Jerusalem were thus 'sold' to the new Jewish settlers. The magnitude of this plunder of Arab refugee property can be appreciated when it is realized, as explained in Chapter 8, that the Arabs owned the greater part of the properties in modern Jerusalem.

The Conciliation Commission asked Israel to abrogate the Absentee Property legislation and to suspend all measures of requisition and occupation of Arab homes and lands. But Israel refused. In 1950, the General Assembly by its resolution 394 (V) directed the Conciliation Commission 'to continue negotiations with the parties concerned regarding measures for the protection of the rights, property and interests of the refugees'. Israel, however, ignored the Conciliation Commission's efforts to protect Arab refugee property.[16]

Unification of Palestine and Jordan

Like Israel, King Abdullah of Jordan was in no way enthusiastic about the internationalization of Jerusalem. He had originally dispatched his army in 1948, in agreement with the other Arab States, to the assistance of the Palestinians and succeeded in thwarting the Jewish onslaught on the Old City of Jerusalem.

But seeing that Israel had rejected the international régime envisaged for Jerusalem and had even proclaimed the city to be its capital, King Abdullah felt no qualms about his incorporating into his kingdom the Old City and other Palestinian territory which his army had occupied. To this end he organized elections in April 1950, in Jordan and in the territories occupied by the Jordanian army in Palestine, for a National Assembly to be composed of an equal number of Palestinians and Jordanians. Then on 24 April the National Assembly convened at Amman and adopted a resolution for the unification of Palestine and Jordan in one state on the basis of a constitutional and parliamentary government. The resolution emphasized that all Arab rights in Palestine shall be safeguarded and that the union shall not prejudice the final settlement of the Palestine question.

The other Arab States did not approve of this action and a resolution was adopted by the League of Arab States which declared that the territories occupied by the Jordanian army in Palestine were to be held in trust for the people of Palestine. With time, however, there was a tacit acceptance by the Arab States of Jordan's action.

Strictly speaking, therefore, the Old City of Jerusalem was not *annexed* in the legal sense by Jordan, but became part of the enlarged kingdom that resulted from the unification of the territories of Palestine and Jordan.

The Old City remained under Jordanian rule until June 1967 when it was captured by Israeli forces.

Notes

1. Folke Bernadotte, *To Jerusalem* (Hodder and Stoughton, London, 1951).
2. UN Doc.A/648, 16 September 1948.
3. Walter Eytan, *The First Ten Years* (Weidenfeld and Nicolson, London, 1958), p. 65.
4. Official Records of the 2nd session of the General Assembly, Ad Hoc Committee, p. 304.
5. UN Doc.A/1367.
6. Official Records of the 3rd session of the General Assembly, Ad Hoc Political Committee, 5 May 1949.
7. Official Records of the General Assembly, Ad Hoc Political Committee, 1949, Part II, pp. 179-360.
8. Official Records of the 3rd session of the General Assembly, Ad Hoc Political Committee, 1949, Part II, p. 223.
9. Article 2, paragraph 7 of the Charter states:

Nothing contained in the present Charter shall authorize the United Nations to intervene in matters which are essentially within the domestic jurisdiction of any state or shall require the Members to submit such matters to settlement under the present Charter: but this principle shall not prejudice the application or enforcement measures under Chapter VII.

10. Official Records, 1949, pp. 286-7 (emphasis added).

11. Ibid., p. 286.

12. Ibid., p. 351.

13. UN Doc.A/648, p. 14.

14. UN Doc.A/922, 21 June 1949.

15. Henry Cattan, *Palestine and International Law*, 2nd edn (Longman, London, 1976), pp. 144 *et seq*.

16. See the Reports of the Conciliation Commission in UN Docs.A/927, 21 June 1949, A/992, 22 September 1949, A/1985, 15 July 1951 and A/3199, 4 October 1956.

Chapter Six

ISRAEL'S CAPTURE OF THE OLD CITY, 1967, AND ITS AFTERMATH

War of 1967

On 5 June 1967 Israel launched a war of aggression against Egypt, Syria and Jordan. In a lightning surprise attack, Israeli aircraft disabled Egypt's fighters and bombers on their aerodromes and Israel's armed forces invaded the Gaza Strip, the Sinai Desert, the Golan region, the Old City of Jerusalem and the West Bank.[1] Despite the issue of several ceasefire orders by the Security Council, Israel pursued its attacks until it achieved its territorial objectives. On the evening of 7 June the Old City of Jerusalem as well as all the rest of the West Bank were in Israeli hands.

Although Israel pretended to the Security Council on 5 June 1967 that it was the victim of aggression and that 'Egyptian land and air forces have moved against Israel and that Israeli forces are now engaged in repelling the Egyptian forces', it is now established that this was a fabricated story intended to cover up Israel's aggression.[2]

The same deceit was practised by Israel to cover up its aggression against Jordan. General Odd Bull, Chief of Staff of the UN Truce Supervision Organization, reports that on 5 June an official of the Israeli Foreign Ministry informed him 'that Egyptian planes had taken off against Israel but had been intercepted by Israeli planes' and asked him 'to transmit a message to King Hussein expressing the hope of the Israeli Government that he would not join in the war. If he stayed out, Israel would not attack him, but if, on the other hand, he chose to come in, Israel would use against him all the means at its disposal.' General Odd Bull continues: 'This was a threat, pure and simple, and it is not the normal practice of the UN to pass on threats from one government to another. But this message was so important that we quickly sent it to King Hussein.'[3]

However, the pretence that Israel would not attack Jordan is belied by the secret decision adopted by the Israeli Cabinet on 4 June 1967 (which was made public on 4 June 1972) to attack Egypt, Syria and Jordan on the following day. It is also belied by Israel's annexation of the Old City in less than three weeks after its capture.

More Refugees

Immediately after their occupation of the Old City, Israeli troops inti-midated the Arab inhabitants in order to force them to leave as in 1948 and to seek refuge in Jordan. Loudspeakers announced the capture of the Old City and asked the Arab inhabitants to leave for Amman 'while the road was still open'. They were told that their safety would not be guaranteed if they remained. In other places, such as in Bethlehem, the people were ordered to leave within two hours, failing which their houses would be blown up over their heads. Some heeded the threats, others did not. In his Report to the Security Council, Mr N.G. Gussing, the Special Representative of the Secretary-General of the UN, men-tioned 'persistent reports of acts of intimidation by Israeli armed forces and of Israeli attempts to suggest to the population, by loudspeakers mounted on cars, that they might be better off on the East Bank. There have also been reports that in several localities buses and trucks were put at the disposal of the population for travel purposes.'[4] Several hundred Arab families were forcibly ousted from their homes in the early days of the capture of the Old City, and buses and trucks took them to Jericho.[5]

The total number of Palestinians from the West Bank, including Jerusalem, who by reason of hostilities or intimidation took refuge in Jordan in June 1967 was estimated by the Government of Jordan at 410,248. Both the Security Council by its resolution 237 of 14 June 1967 and the General Assembly by its resolution 2252 of 4 July 1967 called upon Israel to facilitate the return of those inhabitants who were displaced. In apparent compliance, Israel announced in July 1967 that it would permit the return of the refugees of the last conflict. After prolonged negotiations between the International Red Cross and the Governments of Israel and Jordan and much discussion about rules and procedure, the application forms which Israel required should be sub-mitted by the refugees were issued on 12 August 1967. Notwith-standing the stringent conditions which hemmed in the repatriation programme, 40,000 applications were submitted to Israel for the return of 150,000 Palestinian refugees. The majority of those applications were not approved or even considered. Only a small number, i.e. 14,000, were permitted to return. However, at the same time as this token repatriation was taking place, Israel forced 17,000 Palestinians to leave and to seek refuge on the East Bank.

The number of Palestinians who were displaced in 1967 from their homes in Jerusalem has not been determined with precision. Estimates of the number vary from 7,000 according to the International Red Cross to 30,000 according to other sources.[6] What is certain, however, is that Israel did not permit the repatriation of the refugees whose homes were in Jerusalem. This significant fact is brought to light by the Commissioner-General of UNRWA[7] who reported: 'Among those permitted to return, it appears that there were very few former inhabitants of the Old City of Jerusalem' (UN Doc.A/6713, p. 4). The reason for this veto on the return of the inhabitants of Jerusalem is obvious: the return of the original inhabitants does not fit into the Israeli scheme of judaization of the city.

As to the Palestinians who remained in the Old City, they were subjected to a régime of repression and economic strangulation that was designed to lead them to emigrate and which violated elementary human rights and fundamental freedoms. On 19 December 1968 the General Assembly established a Special Committee to investigate Israel's violations of human rights in the occupied territories, including Jerusalem. Israel, however, did not allow the Special Committee to visit the occupied territories. None the less, the Committee conducted its investigations and reported to the General Assembly that Israel pursued in the occupied territories, including Jerusalem, 'policies and practices which are in violation of the human rights of the population'. The General Assembly has condemned in several resolutions Israel's violations of human rights of the population in the occupied territories, including Jerusalem.[8]

Annexation of the Old City

Although on the first day of the war, Israel's Prime Minister, Levi Eshkol, proclaimed that Israel had no territorial claims and Israel's Defence Minister, Moshe Dayan, declared that 'we have no aim of territorial conquest', Israel proceeded with the annexation of the Old City soon after its capture. On 27 June 1967, it enacted the *Law and Administration Ordinance (Amendment No. 11)* which provided that the law, jurisdiction and administration of the state should apply in any area designated by the Government by order. On the following day the Israeli Government issued an order which declared that an area comprising the Old City of Jerusalem and some adjacent territory shall be subject to the law, jurisdiction and administration of Israel. This meant nothing else but the annexation of the Old City and other designated areas. On the same day the area of the Municipal Corporation of

Jerusalem was enlarged to include the annexed area. This meant an expansion of the municipal area of Jerusalem from 40 to 100 square kilometres. Compared with the *corpus separatum* of Jerusalem as delineated by the UN in 1947, the expanded municipal area remained approximately the same at the east and west, but was extended to the north to include Kalandia airport, and was cut back in the south to exclude the three Arab towns of Bethlehem, Beit Jala and Beit Sahur. In effect, Israel annexed the entirety of the *corpus separatum* of Jerusalem as defined by the UN in 1947 to the exclusion of the three above-mentioned towns. Since then Jerusalem and its surrounding area have been severed politically, administratively and economically from the other territories occupied in June 1967 and have been treated as Israeli territory, except with regard to the national status of the inhabitants who have remained Jordanian citizens despite the annexation.

As in the annexation of modern Jerusalem, Israel attempted at first to deceive world opinion and to explain away the annexation of the Old City as an innocent action possessing no political significance. Repeating almost word for word the assurances that he gave to the Ad Hoc Political Committee in 1949, Abba Eban, Israel's Foreign Minister, who had gained some expertise in the matter, told the General Assembly in June 1967:

> Some delegations and Governments have made statements in recent days concerning certain developments in Jerusalem. There seems to me to be a basic misunderstanding about the import of yesterday's administrative legislation. This, as the General Assembly will be aware, contained no new political statement, and concerned itself exclusively with the urgent necessities of repairing the ravages and dislocations arising from the division of the city's life . . . The import of the recent legislation is to assure for the inhabitants of all parts of the city social, municipal and fiscal services.[9]

However, the General Assembly was not misled by this rhetoric and condemned the annexation in no uncertain terms. Similarly, the Security Council also condemned Israel's annexation and declared it invalid. These condemnations will be referred to in greater detail in Chapter 10.

Despite its initial false statements to the UN about its guiltless intentions with regard to Jerusalem, Israel subsequently made no secret of its annexation of the city which it described as 'integration' and of its determination to maintain it against all odds notwithstanding its condemnation by the UN. Israel even boldly declared that its annexation of Jerusalem is 'irrevocable' and 'not negotiable'.[10]

Israel's action in annexing the Old City should not be equated with Jordan's action in 1950 in proceeding with the unification of Jordanian and Palestinian territories, including Jerusalem. These two actions differ basically in their purpose, legal nature and political significance. Israel's action was plainly an aggression and a usurpation of Arab territory by a foreign people. Jordan's action was taken with the consent of the Palestinians and did not involve their subjugation, displacement or dispossession. In accordance with the constitution adopted for the unified territories of Jordan and Palestine, the National Assembly was constituted of an equal number of Jordanians and Palestinians. Hence, Jordan's action was neither an aggression nor a usurpation.

Threats, Desecrations and Vandalism

Intoxicated by their capture of the Old City, some prominent officers of the Government caused world concern by asserting claims against Islamic Holy Places in Jerusalem and Hebron. Ambassador E. Thalmann of Switzerland, charged by the Secretary-General of the UN with a fact-finding mission on the situation in Jerusalem, reported:

> Statements by Israel official representatives and Jewish personalities concerning Jewish claims and plans in the Temple area had an alarming effect.[11]

The Israeli Minister for Religious Affairs was reported to have declared at a press conference at Jerusalem on 12 August 1967 that the authorities considered the site of the Mosque of Omar as their property 'by past acquisition or by conquest'[12] and that there was question of rebuilding the Temple of Solomon in the area of the *Haram Al-Sharif*. He is also reported to have said:

> As to the Holy Ibrahimi Mosque, the Cave is a Jewish shrine which we have bought, in the same way that we bought the Holy Rock in the days of David and the Jebusites, and our rights in the Cave and the Rock are rights of conquest and acquisition.[13]

The matter did not rest at ominous threats but soon evolved into provocative acts. Ambassador Thalmann reported:

Most of the Arabs interviewed by the Personal Representative stated that the Moslem population was shocked by Israeli acts which violated the sanctity of the Moslem shrines. It was regarded as a particular provocation that the Chief Rabbi of the Israel Army, with others of his faith, conducted prayers in the area of the *Haram Al-Sharif*. [The Israel Government has in the meantime put a stop to the offering of further prayers by members of the Jewish faith in the area of the Holy Mosque.] [14]

Despite the ban, however, the example set by the Chief Rabbi of the Army was followed in 1975 by some forty youths who celebrated the anniversary of Israel's independence by holding a religious service and singing Hebrew songs in the area of the *Haram Al-Sharif*. Charged with a violation of the ban, the accused were acquitted by the Magistrate who held the Jews had a right to pray on Temple Mount. A higher court left the decision on the right of Jews to pray there in the hands of the Minister of Religion. The ban, however, has continued, though it has not prevented fights between nationalist and religious Jews over the holding of religious services in the area of the *Haram Al-Sharif*.

Another outrage which shocked world opinion and was strongly condemned by the Security Council was the arson committed on 21 August 1969 at the Mosque of Al-Aqsa. Extensive damage was caused to the roof of this shrine and an historic twelfth-century carved wooden pulpit was gutted by the fire. Although the Israeli authorities arrested and tried the culprit — an Australian — and later deported him as mentally deranged, Islamic world opinion considered Israel's occupation of Jerusalem and its Holy Places and the campaign conducted in certain Jewish circles for the restoration of Solomon's Temple on the site of the *Haram Al-Sharif* to have inspired and largely contributed to this grave act of vandalism. In fact, the culprit is reported to have told the Israeli authorities that his purpose was to burn the Mosque of Al-Aqsa so that the Temple of Solomon could be built on its site.

Christian Holy Places also were not spared and there have been desecrations of shrines, religious property and cemeteries on Mount Zion. The Tombs of the Patriarchs in the courtyard of the Armenian Church of St Saviour were broken into and their bones scattered about. [15]

The Israeli authorities also attempted to interfere with the exercise of religious rights and practices by Moslems and Christians. Thus they sought to assume jurisdiction over Moslem religious courts. They also sought to censor religious preaching on Fridays in the mosques. [16] Similarly, they attempted to prevent access by Christians to the Cenacle on

Saturdays, the day of the Jewish Sabbath. These interferences with religious rights and practices met with the opposition of the communities concerned and were abandoned by the Israeli authorities.

Equally offensive was the disrespect shown by some Israelis to the Holy Places of the two other communities:

> The Christian Arab complained that reports of smoking, loud talk, improper dress, and dogs in the Church of the Holy Sepulchre were not compatible with the sacred character of the site; and the Muslim Arab complained that mini-skirts, embraces between the sexes, and holding a fashion show against the background of Al-Aqsa Mosque were not in keeping with the character of the Holy Places.[17]

More recently Christian clergymen were harassed and church property in Jerusalem was vandalized in a series of attacks on Baptists, Roman Catholics and Russian Orthodox.[18] 'It is a Jewish obligation to destroy graven images. The Christians have no place in Jerusalem, which is the Jewish capital' declared one of those detained for vandalism at Christian sites.[19] As a result, the Christian communities protested against the relative immunity which the authors of such vandalism seem to enjoy and declared that such acts are caused by 'an exclusivist conception of the character of Jerusalem'.[20]

Demolitions and Excavations

During the first week of their occupation of the Old City, the Israelis razed to the ground the historic Mughrabi quarter which dated back to AD 1320, destroying, in the words of David Hirst, 'seven hundred years of Muslim history' in order to make a parking lot in front of the Wailing Wall. Similarly, a large area of the historic cemetery of Mamillah which contained the tombs of many famous or pious Moslems was bulldozed and converted into a car park. Ambassador Thalmann mentions that the dynamiting and bulldozing of 135 houses in the Mughrabi quarter involved the expulsion of 650 poor and pious Moslems from their homes.[21] There was also a number of other demolitions of Arab-owned buildings in and around the Old City.[22]

In addition to demolitions, in an attempt to search for ancient Jewish vestiges, the Israeli authorities undertook extensive excavations in the vicinity of the *Haram Al-Sharif*.[23] As these acts endangered Moslem Holy Places, vigorous protests were made by the Moslems. In several resolutions, the General Assembly and the Security Council censured Israel for its archaeological excavations and appealed to it — without avail — to preserve the historical and religious heritage in the city.

Similarly, the UN Educational, Scientific and Cultural Organization (UNESCO) showed great concern over Israel's actions in Jerusalem. Since 1968 UNESCO has repeatedly called on Israel to desist from its excavations in Jerusalem and from the alteration of its features or its cultural and historical character, but again without avail. In 1974, 1976 and 1978 UNESCO condemned Israel's persistence in altering the historical features of Jerusalem.

The damage done to the historical and religious heritage in Jerusalem by Israel's destructions and excavations in the Old City was described by Mr René Maheu, former Director-General of UNESCO, in these terms:

Between the summer of 1967 and the summer of 1969 the western side of the sacred enclosure [*Haram Al-Sharif*] called the Wailing Wall, was cleared over a distance of 140 metres, and a vast esplanade was opened in front of the Wall by destroying a medieval quarter which formed part of the traditional urban structure of the Old City. Besides, this quarter contained some buildings of architectural value or of undoubted cultural character . . . The works undertaken on this site of the Old City have robbed it of its picturesqueness and have given it the appearance of a gaping wound in the flesh of the City . . . Again in order to clear the sacred enclosure, tunnels were dug in 1970-1971 over a distance of 215 metres. But certain movements of the earth above these tunnels were observed which are likely to put in danger the buildings in the quarter overhead . . . Beyond these particular aspects, the greatest danger which threatens Jerusalem in its entirety is an erratic urbanization of a modern style like that which has disfigured so many ancient cities in various countries . . . The alterations that have occurred since 1967 in the sites and the appearance of the City are very grave. If such evolution were to be pursued, the personality of Jerusalem, its unique charm, the extraordinary physical radiance of its spirituality, would be doomed within a short time.[24]

Disfigurement of the City

The massive colonization of Jerusalem and its surroundings has resulted in the erection of clusters of hideous concrete structures which have disfigured the Holy City and its skyline. As a result, Jerusalem has been changed almost out of recognition and its charm and beauty have now been lost for ever. The Archbishop of Canterbury, the Right Reverend Michael Ramsey, said in condemning the disfigurement of Jerusalem:

It is distressing indeed that the building programme of the present authorities is disfiguring the city and its surroundings in ways which wound the feelings of those who care for its historic beauty and suggest an insensitive attempt to proclaim as an Israeli city one which can never be other than the city of three great religions and their peoples.[25]

In a letter to *The Times* on 14 March 1971 Arnold Toynbee and Geoffrey Furlonge referred to 'the imminent danger that by the construction for political reasons of ill-considered housing developments on expropriated Arab land, the Israelis will do irreparable harm to the unique character and beauty of the Holy City'.

Despite these warnings, the disfigurement of Jerusalem is still proceeding by leaps and bounds in execution of the Israeli colonization programme which will be discussed in the next chapter.

Notes

1. The name 'West Bank' which means the west bank of the Jordan River that separated Palestine from Transjordan is completely inaccurate and unhistorical. This name was coined by Jordan in order to describe the territory of Palestine which it occupied in 1948 as opposed to the east bank of the Jordan River which was known as Transjordan.

2. See Henry Cattan, *Palestine and International Law*, 2nd edn (Longman, London, 1976), pp. 168-72.

3. General Odd Bull, *War and Peace in the Middle East* (Leo Cooper, London, 1976), p. 113.

4. UN Doc.A/6797, 13 September 1967, p. 13.

5. *Washington Post*, 20 June 1967.

6. Richard H. Pfaff, *Jerusalem: Keystone of an Arab-Israeli Settlement* (American Enterprise Institute for Public Policy Research, Washington DC, 1969), p. 36.

7. UNRWA is the abbreviated name of the United Nations Relief and Works Agency for Palestine Refugees.

8. See, *inter alia*, General Assembly resolutions dated 20 December 1971, 15 December 1972, 15 December 1975 and the resolutions of the Commission on

Human Rights of 21 February 1979 and 13 February 1980.

9. 1541st meeting of the General Assembly, 29 June 1967.

10. UN Docs.6793 and S/8146, 12 September 1967.

11. UN Doc.6793, p. 21.

12. The term 'past acquisition' refers to the Jewish tradition that David purchased from a Jebusite the land on which Solomon's Temple was built.

13. UN Doc.6793, p. 53. The Ibrahimi Mosque is located in Hebron and contains the cave of Machpelah in which are buried Abraham, Sarah and Jacob. The Rock refers to the Rock over which the Mosque of the Dome of the Rock is built.

14. UN Doc.A/6793, p. 21.

15. A list of protests made by religious institutions to the Israeli authorities against desecrations of Holy Places is set out in Jordan's communication to the UN: Doc.S/9001, 19 April 1968.

16. UN Doc.A/6793 and H.E. Bovis, *The Jerusalem Question* (Stanford, California, 1971), p. 107.

17. Pfaff, *Jerusalem: Keystone*, p. 45.

18. *International Herald Tribune*, 29 January 1980.

19. *The Times*, 2 February 1980.

20. Translation from *Le Monde*, 9 February 1980.

21. UN Doc.6793, p. 21.

22. See the various complaints made by Jordan to the Security Council, and in particular, UN Docs.S/9001, S/9197, S/9284 and S/10882.

23. Rouhi Al-Khatib, *The Judaization of Jerusalem* (Research Centre, Beirut, 1972), pp. 19-20. See also Jordan's complaints to the UN concerning excavations in UN Doc.S/10169, S/10882 and S/11246.

24. Translation from *Le Monde*, 21 November 1974.

25. *Diocesan Newsletter*, January 1971.

Chapter Seven

THE MASSIVE COLONIZATION OF JERUSALEM AND ITS SURROUNDINGS

Colonization Since 1948

Immediately following the occupation of modern Jerusalem and the western part of the *corpus separatum* in 1948, Israel undertook a massive colonization of these areas without the least regard to the rights of their Arab owners or the international régime prescribed for the City of Jerusalem. As previously mentioned in Chapter 5, all the lands and homes of the Arabs in modern Jerusalem were confiscated and filled with Jewish settlers and immigrants.

The Arab villages of Ein Karem, Deir Yassin, Kalonia (part of Motza on the map), El Malha and Lifta (a suburb of Jerusalem), all located in the western section of the *corpus separatum*, were destroyed and razed to the ground so that their Arab inhabitants who were displaced by the massacre of Deir Yassin would be unable to return to them. The names of these villages which appear on the map of the City of Jerusalem annexed to resolution 181 (II) have now passed into history as the villages themselves have disappeared without any trace. The whole area has been occupied by the Jewish settlers that Israel was anxious to bring to Jerusalem.

As a result, the Jewish population of the *corpus separatum* of Jerusalem which stood at 99,690 in 1947 rose to 194,000 in 1967.

Colonization Since 1967

An equally feverish and massive colonization of Jerusalem and its surroundings, which were previously under Jordanian control, was undertaken by Israel on Arab land after the capture of the Old City. Land which belonged to Arab refugees was confiscated while land whose owners were present was nominally expropriated, but was, in fact, confiscated. According to Israeli figures, the areas expropriated in Jerusalem and its environs between 1967 and 1974 amounted to 18,000 *dunoms* (4,444 acres).[1] Since then many other expropriations have taken place.[2] By the beginning of 1978, 30 acres representing one-sixth of the Old City had been expropriated.[3] In all cases, the owners thus robbed invariably refused the derisory compensation offered for the forcible misappropriation of their property since they considered their dispossession to be null and void.

In the first inquiry ever undertaken by the UN specifically with regard to Israel's colonization of the territories occupied in 1967, including Jerusalem, certain important facts were brought to light. The inquiry was conducted by a Commission appointed in accordance with the resolution of the Security Council No. 446 of 22 March 1979 'to examine the situation relating to settlements in the Arab territories occupied since 1967, including Jerusalem'. In its Report dated 12 July 1979 (S/13450), the Commission mentions that 17 settlements were established in and around Jerusalem. In the Old City, 320 housing units were established for Jews, 160 Arab houses destroyed, 600 homes expropriated and 6,500 Arab residents evacuated.

It should be remarked that the Commission reported only on the settlements established since 1967 but not on settlements established prior to that date in the area of the *corpus separatum* because its terms of reference were limited to reporting on the former.

It is evident from the Commission's Report that Jewish settlement in and around Jerusalem was more intensive than in other occupied areas. The Commission states that the number of settlers in Jerusalem and the West Bank has reached 90,000. The Commission gives no breakdown of this figure, but it seems that the largest number of those 90,000 settlers are found in the Jerusalem area. According to well-informed sources, the number of settlers in the eastern part of Jerusalem alone has reached 80,000 while the number of settlers in other settlements in the West Bank amount to about 10,000.

As a result of such intensive settlement, the demographic structure of Jerusalem has now been radically altered. The Arab population of the *corpus separatum* which stood in 1947 at 105,540 according to UN figures has now been reduced to about 75,000 while the Jewish population which was then estimated at 99,690 now exceeds 275,000.

Israel has made no secret of its plan to attract and settle in Jerusalem hundreds of thousands of Jewish immigrants. The purpose of such intensive settlement is twofold: political, so as to judaize completely the population of the City, and military, so as to encircle it with fortress-like buildings inhabited by Jews.

The following excerpts from the Report show the magnitude and implications of Israeli settlement:

222. The land seized by the Israeli authorities as a whole, either

specifically for the establishment of those settlements or for other stated reasons, covers 27 per cent of the occupied West Bank . . .

229. The Commission is of the view that a correlation exists between the establishment of Israeli settlements and the displacement of the Arab population. Thus it was reported that since 1967, when that policy started, the Arab population has been reduced by 32 per cent in Jerusalem and the West Bank . . .

230. The Commission is convinced that in the implementation of its policy of settlements, Israel has resorted to methods — often coercive and sometimes more subtle — which included the control of water resources, the seizure of private properties, the destruction of houses, and the banishment of persons, and has shown disregard for basic human rights, including in particular the right of the refugees to return to their homeland.

231. For the Arab inhabitants still living in those territories, particularly in Jerusalem and the West Bank, they are subjected to continuous pressure to emigrate in order to make room for new settlers who, by contrast, are encouraged to come to the area . . .

233. The Commission considers that the pattern of that settlement policy, as a consequence, is causing profound and irreversible changes of a geographical and demographic nature in those territories, including Jerusalem.

234. The Commission has no doubt that those changes are of such a profound nature that they constitute a violation of the fourth Geneva Convention relative to the Protection of Civilian Persons in Time of War of 12 August 1949 and of the relevant decisions adopted by the United Nations in the matter, more specifically: Security Council resolutions 237 (1967) of 14 June 1967, 252 (1968) of 21 May 1968 and 298 (1971) of 25 September 1971; the consensus statement by the President of the Security Council on 11 November 1976; as well as General Assembly resolutions 2253 (ES-V) and 2254 (ES-V) of 4 and 14 July 1967, 32/5 of 28 October 1977, and 33/113 of 18 December 1978.

UN Condemnations of Settlements

Since 1967, the UN has deplored or condemned the establishment by Israel of settlements in the occupied territories, including Jerusalem, and has declared that Israel's actions in this regard have no legal validity. The UN also condemned the concomitant operations to which Israel has recourse for the creation of settlements, namely the expropriations and confiscations of land and the transfer of an alien population to the occupied territories. The principal resolutions in this respect were referred to in the above-quoted Report of the Commission.

A recent and more severe condemnation of Israeli settlements was pronounced by the Security Council on 1 March 1980 in resolution 465 as a result of an Israeli plan to colonize the Arab city of Hebron. The resolution stated, *inter alia*, that the Security Council

5. *Determines* that all measures taken by Israel to change the physical character, demographic composition, institutional structure or status of the Palestinian and other Arab territories occupied since 1967, including Jerusalem, or any part thereof, have no legal validity and that Israel's policy and practices of settling parts of its population and new immigrants in those territories constitute a flagrant violation of the Fourth Geneva Convention relative to the Protection of Civilian Persons in Time of War and also constitute a serious obstruction to achieving a comprehensive, just and lasting peace in the Middle East;

6. *Strongly deplores* the continuation and persistence of Israel in pursuing those policies and practices and calls upon the Government and people of Israel to rescind those measures, to dismantle the existing settlements and in particular to cease, on an urgent basis, the establishment, construction and planning of settlements in the Arab territories occupied since 1967, including Jerusalem;

7. *Calls upon* all States not to provide Israel with any assistance to be used specifically in connexion with settlements in the occupied territories.

Resolution 465 possessed two new features that distinguished it from previous UN condemnations of settlements.

First, it received the support of the US Government which, in the past, despite its public declarations condemning Israeli settlements as being illegal and contrary to international law, had usually abstained from supporting similar resolutions of the Security Council and the General Assembly.

Second, unlike previous resolutions which merely censured, deplored or condemned settlements, this last resolution called, in addition, for the dismantling of all settlements in the occupied territories, including Jerusalem.

It is noteworthy that Paragraph 5 of the resolution reaffirms the legal invalidity of measures taken by Israel in Palestinian and other Arab territories occupied since 1967, including Jerusalem, 'or any part thereof'. This language would seem to cover Israel's actions in the Old City and in modern Jerusalem.

President Carter's Reversal

The progress achieved by resolution 465 in the US position on Israeli settlements was, however, blasted two days later by President Carter in an extraordinary statement issued by the White House on 3 March which disavowed US concurrence to the resolution. In his statement, President Carter reaffirmed his opposition to Israeli settlements in the occupied territories though he made strenuous efforts, he pointed out, to eliminate from the resolution the reference to their dismantlement. He declared that the US vote in the Security Council 'does not represent a change in our position regarding the Israeli settlements in the occupied areas nor regarding the status of Jerusalem . . . As to Jerusalem, we strongly believe that it should be undivided . . . and that its status should be determined in negotiations for a comprehensive peace settlement.' He emphasized that

> The United States vote in the United Nations was approved with the understanding that all references to Jerusalem would be deleted. The failure to communicate this clearly resulted in a vote in favor of the resolution rather than abstention.

One may doubt whether this reversal in the President's position was, in fact, due to a failure of communication or simply to a failure of nerves in the face of the uproar raised against the resolution by Israel and the Jewish lobby, a fact which would influence the Jewish vote in the presidential elections. The latter explanation receives support from the concluding paragraph of the statement:

> I want to reiterate in the most unequivocal of terms that in the autonomy negotiations and in other fora, the United States will neither support nor accept any position that might jeopardize Israel's vital security interests. Our commitment to Israel's security and well-being remains unqualified and unshakable.

President Carter's distinction between settlements in the occupied territories which he opposed, and settlements in Jerusalem in regard to which he wanted to delete all references in the resolution, can mean only one thing: acquiescence in Israel's continued colonization of Jerusalem. As to his view that the status of Jerusalem should be determined in negotiations for a comprehensive peace settlement, this surely should not prevent the condemnation of settlements in the city which, from the standpoint of their illegality, are on the same footing as other settlements. No reason exists to permit Israel to continue with the creation of settlements in Jerusalem. The silence in this regard would have the effect of encouraging Israel to pursue its colonization and to change the physical, demographic and political realities in the city.

Moreover, the President's statement that Jerusalem 'should be undivided' raises some queries about his intentions. Does he mean that Jerusalem should be subject to an international régime as envisaged by the UN in 1947? Or does he mean that it should be wholly under Israeli sovereignty – as claimed by Israel?

President Carter's disavowal of the US vote in favour of resolution 465 had immediate consequences. It encouraged the Israeli Knesset to denounce on 6 March the resolution and to reaffirm Israel's 'right' to settle Jews anywhere in the occupied territories. Another consequence was that 'the Israeli Government, in defiance of mounting international criticism, expropriated on 11 March 1000 acres of Arab land east of Jerusalem in order to close a circle of Jewish suburbs around the city'.[4] A still further consequence was that the Israeli Government decided to establish two religious schools in Hebron, a move that had precipitated the condemnation of Israel's settlements by the Security Council in resolution 465.

Considering that President Carter disavowed, for what were obviously electoral reasons, the US support of the UN condemnation of Israeli settlements in Jerusalem, it is no surprise to find his main opponents in the elections also exploiting the question of Jerusalem and Israeli settlements. Thus in a meeting with Orthodox rabbis at Brooklyn on 24 March, Senator Edward Kennedy was reported to have waved in the air a copy of the Security Council resolution of 1 March and stated that all of it, not just a paragraph or two, was unacceptable. On the same day, in a meeting with Jewish leaders in New York, Mr Ronald Reagan was asked about President Carter's statement that Jerusalem should be undivided and where did he stand on the question of sovereignty? His reply was: 'An undivided city of Jerusalem means sovereignty for Israel over that city.'[5]

It is a matter for deep regret and serious concern that the question of Jerusalem should thus become the subject of political auction among American presidential candidates.

Illegality of Settlements

The creation of settlements in and around Jerusalem is unlawful under UN resolutions and international law.

On the one hand, the establishment by Israel of settlements in the *corpus separatum* of Jerusalem is a flagrant violation of General Assembly resolutions 181 (II), 194 (III) and 303 (IV) which have laid down an international régime for the City of Jerusalem. The establishment of settlements in and around Jerusalem in the territory occupied in 1967 violates in addition a number of UN resolutions which have condemned their creation.

On the other hand, the establishment of settlements in occupied territory violates international law and the Fourth Geneva Convention of 12 August 1949. Being a belligerent occupier, Israel possesses no right to seize or confiscate Arab property and build settlements thereon. A belligerent occupier exercises only a temporary power of administration, solely for military purposes, and cannot act as a sovereign, annex or colonize occupied territory.

As to the two arguments on which Israel relies for its colonization of occupied territory, namely a 'biblical' right to settle the land of Palestine and a right to establish settlements for 'security reasons', the first is an absurdity and the second is a fake. The argument that Israel needs to establish settlements for 'security reasons' is simply a pretext for its refusal to withdraw from occupied territory or for its annexation. If anyone needs security, it is surely Israel's neighbours who need protection against its repeated aggressions.

The scandalous recourse by the Israeli Government to 'security reasons' as a pretext for confiscating Arab land for settlement was exposed by the Israeli High Court of Justice on 22 October 1979 when it held that the land which was seized for the creation of the new settlement of Elon Moreh near Nablus was taken for 'political reasons' and not for 'security needs' as claimed by the Government. The High Court further rejected the contention made by the promoters of the settlement (Gush Emunim) that the Jews possess a 'biblical' right to settle in the West Bank. The Court also ordered the dismantling of the settlement.

In response to the Court's ruling, the Government stated that it would move the settlement to state domain or public land. Here again the taking of state domain or public land for the creation of Jewish settlements is as unlawful as the appropriation of privately owned land. This for two reasons. First, state domain was registered in Palestine in the name of the High Commissioner in trust for the Government of Palestine. Many lands, however, which were not by destination public lands, such as the common land of villages, whether used for cultivation or grazing, were also registered in the name of the High Commissioner who held them in trust for the villagers. The second reason is that even in the case of strictly state domain destined for public use, its seizure by a belligerent occupier is not authorized by international law. Enemy public property in territory under military occupation 'may be used (for example, occupied or used to produce food or timber) but not acquired or disposed of'.[6] Oppenheim states the rule in these terms:

> 134. Appropriation of public immoveables is not lawful so long as the territory on which they are found has not become State property of the occupant through annexation. During mere military occupation of enemy territory, a belligerent may not sell, or otherwise alienate, public enemy land and buildings, but may only appropriate their produce. Article 55 of the Hague Regulations expressly enacts that a belligerent occupying enemy territory shall only be regarded as administrator and usufructuary of the public buildings, real property, forests and agricultural works belonging to the hostile State and situated in the occupied territory . . .[7]

In establishing settlements in and around Jerusalem, Israel has acted as if it were a sovereign or the successor to the previous sovereign. In accordance with international law, Israel is neither a sovereign nor a successor to the previous sovereign.

Israel cannot claim that it is a successor to the Administration of Palestine. In accordance with resolution 181 (II) of 29 November 1947 the assets of the Administration of Palestine were allocated between the Arab and Jewish States and the City of Jerusalem. As regards immoveables, Part I (E) stated: 'Immovable assets shall become the property of the government of the territory in which they are situated.'

Hence, even if one assumes that despite the grave irregularities in its creation which affect its legitimacy,[8] Israel could claim to be the successor to the Administration of Palestine in regard to its immovable assets, such a claim must perforce be limited to those assets as are situated within the area of the Jewish State as defined and delimited by resolution 181 (II). On no account can Israel lay claim to immovable assets situated in the territory of the Arab State as delimited by the resolution, regardless of whether any part of this territory was occupied in 1948 or 1967. Nor can Israel lay claim to immovable assets situated in the *corpus separatum* of Jerusalem, regardless of whether any part of it was seized in 1948 or 1967. There exists no basis in international law for the acquisition by Israel in either case of any title to such immovable assets. Hence, Israel is not justified in undertaking the colonization of state domain in territories that lie outside the boundaries of the Jewish State as defined by the UN in 1947.

Notes

1. *Yediot Aharanot*, 29 March 1974.

2. *Monde Diplomatique*, June 1977.

3. Nafez Y. Nazzal, 'The Encirclement of Jerusalem', *Middle East International*, February 1978, p. 18.

4. *International Herald Tribune*, 12 March 1980.

5. Ibid., 25 March 1980.

6. J.G. Starke, *International Law*, 5th edn (Butterworth, London, 1963), p. 411.

7. L. Oppenheim, *International Law*, 7th edn, Vol. 2 (Longman, London, 1952), p. 397.

8. As to which, see Henry Cattan, *Palestine and International Law*, 2nd edn (Longman, London, 1976), pp. 91 *et seq*.

Chapter Eight

THE JUDAIZATION OF JERUSALEM: ITS SIGNIFICANCE AND PERILS

Curtain Over Past History

In order to appreciate the significance and enormity of Israel's judaization of Jerusalem which has been carried out by forcibly altering the facts of dominion, demography and land ownership, it is necessary to view them in perspective against the historical background of the city. This is all the more necessary because Israel has sought to obliterate the Arab and Christian character of Jerusalem and to draw a curtain over its past history. Father Joseph L. Ryan observes: 'As a result of Zionist presentations, the impression is at times given — and taken — that history of any consequence stopped in Palestine in the year 70 A.D. and only began again with the Zionist movement under Herzl.'[1] In effect, by judaizing Jerusalem, Israel has made the world believe that it is merely recovering a city which belongs to the Jews as if nothing had taken place during their two thousand years' absence from it.

The Judaization of Jerusalem is an Anachronism

Israel's annexation of Jerusalem in the middle of the twentieth century under the pretext of resurrecting the capital of a Jewish kingdom that existed in biblical times some 3,000 years ago is reallyⱼnothingⱼbut a political exhumation and obvious usurpation.

Jewish rule in Jerusalem, as we have seen, was of short duration and lasted less than Arab or Christian rule. The unified kingdom established by David remained only seventy-three years. After Solomon, the kingdom of Judah was semi-independent as it paid tribute to Babylon and Egypt. After its destruction in 587 BC, Jewish rule ceased in Jerusalem. The revolts of the Maccabees against the Greeks and the two revolts against the Romans did not restore Jewish sovereignty in Jerusalem.

Christian rule, Byzantine, Crusader and British during the mandate, lasted 429 years while Moslem rule, Arab and Turkish, remained twelve centuries.

It is obvious that Jewish rule in Jerusalem was an ancient and transient episode in the history of the city which cannot justify its seizure and annexation thirty centuries later. If an historic connection were to be accepted as a basis for a territorial claim, the better title would no doubt belong to the Arabs and the Christians, and more particularly the Palestinians, who have had a much longer and more continuous connection with Jerusalem than any other people.

Moreover, Israel's claim to annex Jerusalem on the basis of an historical connection is spurious in fact and in law.

In contrast with the transient presence of the Jews in Jerusalem during biblical times, the Palestinians have continuously lived in the city since its founding by their ancestors, the Canaanites. The Palestinians are its original and indigenous inhabitants and they continued to live in it even after its capture by David. They were not displaced from it by subsequent invaders, except by the Israelis in 1948.

In contrast to the Palestinians, the Jews came to Jerusalem as invaders and were driven away from it by other invaders. After their deportation eighteen centuries ago, they almost completely disappeared from the city until the nineteenth century.

It seems necessary to emphasize that the Jews who, under the Zionist impulse, began to emigrate to Palestine in the latter half of the nineteenth century and who seized in our time Palestine and established the State of Israel are not the descendants of the Israelites who were deported by Babylon or Rome. In other terms, the Israelis who live in Jerusalem today have no racial link with the biblical Israelites. Joseph Reinach explains that most of today's Jews in Palestine have no connection with this country:

> The Jews of Palestinian origin constitute an insignificant minority. Like Christians and Moslems, the Jews have engaged with great zeal in the conversion of people to their faith. Before the Christian era, the Jews had converted to the monotheistic religion of Moses other Semites (or Arabs), Greeks, Egyptians, and Romans in large numbers. Later, Jewish proselytism was not less active in Asia, in the whole of North Africa, in Italy, in Spain and in Gaul. Converted Romans and Gauls no doubt predominated in the Jewish communities mentioned in chronicles of Grégoire de Tours. There were many converted Iberians among the Jews who were expelled from Spain by Ferdinand the Catholic and who spread to Italy, France, the East and Smyrna. The great majority of Russian, Polish and Galician Jews descend from the Khazars, a Tartar people of Southern Russia who were converted in a body to Judaism at the time of Charlemagne. To

speak of a Jewish race, one must be either ignorant or of bad faith. There was a Semitic or Arab race; but there never was a Jewish race.[2]

On the other hand, the State of Israel which came into existence purportedly under a resolution of the UN cannot possibly claim to be the successor of a Jewish biblical monarchy. State succession occurs in international law when, as a result of cession, conquest, union or federation, a state *follows* its predecessor in the possession of its territory. Israel which was established in 1948 did not follow a biblical monarchy in the possession of the territory of Palestine. It is separated from the last biblical monarchy by twenty-five centuries. There exists no rule of international law that recognizes a right of succession by a state created in the twentieth century to a state that existed twenty-five or thirty centuries earlier.

The revival of Jewish rule in Jerusalem in our time is an anachronism and an affront to history, international law and UN resolutions.

Judaization of the Population

Jerusalem lost completely its Jewish population for eighteen centuries. Except for a short period during the reign of Julian the Apostate, the prohibition of the presence of Jews in Jerusalem decreed by Hadrian and renewed by Constantine in 325 and by Heraclius in 628 lasted for several centuries until it was relaxed by the Arabs after their capture of the city. But despite the abrogation of the prohibition, very few Jews lived in Jerusalem. M. Franco, who made a special study of the situation of the Jews in the Ottoman Empire, mentions that the famous Spanish traveller Benjamin of Tudela found 200 Jews in Jerusalem in the year 1173. In 1180 another traveller, Petahia of Ratisbon, found in Jerusalem one coreligionist only. In 1267 a Spanish rabbi, Moïse Ben Nahman, found two Jews in the city.[3]

In consequence of the persecution of the Jews in Western Europe and their expulsion from Spain (1492) and Portugal (1496), some of them sought refuge in Palestine and in other Mediterranean countries. As a result, some Jews came to live in Jerusalem. According to Rappoport, there were 70 Jewish families in Jerusalem in 1488, 200 families in 1495 and 1,500 families in 1521.[4]

In the nineteenth century, the Jewish population of Jerusalem began to increase. According to the Rev. Edward Robinson, Professor of

Biblical Literature at the Union Theological Seminary of New York, who visited Jerusalem in 1838, the population of the city was 11,000 made up as follows:[5]

Moslems	4,500
Christians	3,500
Jews	3,000
Total	11,000

Following the Russian pogroms of 1881 and 1882, a number of Jews emigrated to Palestine and settled in Tiberias, Safed and Jerusalem. In 1917 the Jewish population of Jerusalem numbered 30,000.[6] In 1922, according to the census of the Government of Palestine, the Jewish population of Jerusalem reached 33,971 out of a total population of 62,578 in the urban area of Jerusalem. The 1931 census shows an increase of the Jewish population to 51,222 out of a total population of 90,503 within the municipal limits of the city. At the end of 1946 the Jewish population of the City of Jerusalem, envisaged by the UN as a *corpus separatum*, had risen to 99,690 compared with 105,540 non-Jews as shown by the following table prepared by the UN:[7]

Moslems	Christians	Others	Total number of Arabs and others	Jews	Total
60,560	44,850	130	105,540	99,690	205,230

The increase in population figures which appears in the UN estimate is explained by the fact that the *corpus separatum* included the inhabitants living within its area which was more extensive than the urban area of Jerusalem.

At the same date, the percentage of Jews to the total population in the sub-district[8] of Jerusalem was only 38 per cent.[9]

The figures of the Jewish population of Jerusalem have been adduced here in order to disprove the Zionist contention that during the last century the Jews constituted the majority of the population. The increase in the number of Jews in Jerusalem occurred only during the British mandate which imposed a massive Jewish immigration into Palestine against the will of its inhabitants. Moreover, the largest number of the Jews who lived in Jerusalem were aliens. Official statistics of the Government of Palestine indicate that in 1944-5 only one-third of the Jewish immigrants had acquired Palestinian citizenship.[10] Consequently, one can consider that, at all material times before the creation of the State of Israel, the Jews who possessed Palestinian nationality were a minority of the population in Jerusalem.

We have seen that the demographic structure in Jerusalem has now been radically altered, the Arab population decreasing to some 75,000 and the Jewish population increasing to about 275,000.

The decrease in the Arab population of Jerusalem has been more pronounced among the Christian Arabs who form the earliest and oldest Christian community in the world. Their number has decreased from the figure of 44,850 at which it stood in 1946 to less than 10,000 at the present day so that the Christian community of Jerusalem has dwindled down to one-quarter of its strength, the remainder having been displaced since the creation of Israel. As a result, Jerusalem, the capital of Christendom, is being gradually de-Christianized. Pope Paul VI expressed his grave concern on 25 March 1974 over the diminution of the number of Christians in Jerusalem, and said:

These Christians are the successors of the ancient and very first Church that gave birth to all other Churches. If their presence were to come to an end, the warmth of a living testimony at the sanctuaries would be extinguished and the Holy Places of Jerusalem would become museums.

Usurpation of Arab Land

The third measure taken by Israel for the judaization of Jerusalem was the dispossession of the original Arab inhabitants and the usurpation of their lands and houses, as previously mentioned.

From the time that the Jews began their colonization in Palestine at the end of the nineteenth century until 1948, all the lands they were able to acquire represented a very small fraction of the area of the country. The Palestine Government's *Village Statistics* show that in 1946 the Jews owned 1,491,699 *dunoms*[11] in Palestine[12] which represented no more than 5.66 per cent of the total area of the country, the rest consisting of public domain, a large part of which was village common land.

In Jerusalem itself, the Jews own an insignificant part of the Old City (less than one per cent) and slightly over one-quarter of modern Jerusalem. Some people commit the gross error of thinking that modern Jerusalem was in 1948 wholly or mostly Jewish-owned. This error can be dissipated by an examination of the municipal map of

Jerusalem which shows the various Arab quarters that existed in modern Jerusalem in 1948 (Appendix V). It was because of the existence of Arab and Jewish quarters in the New City that General Assembly resolution 181 (II) of 1947 recommended the establishment of special town units consisting of the Jewish and Arab sections of new Jerusalem (Section C of Part III of the resolution).

The exact percentages of Arab and Jewish land ownership in the urban area of Jerusalem in 1948 were calculated by Sami Hadawi, a former Government officer of the Department of Land Settlement, on the basis of survey maps and taxation records. These percentages are as follows:

In the Old City which has an area of 800 *dunoms* (197 acres), Jewish ownership is less than 5 *dunoms*. The rest is owned by Moslem and Christian individuals or religious communities, or is *waqf* (religious endowment) for Moslems and Christians.

In modern Jerusalem which has an area of 19,331 *dunoms* (4,773 acres), land ownership is as follows:[13]

Arab-owned	40.00%
Jewish-owned	26.12%
Others (Christian communities)	13.86%
Government and municipal	2.90%
Roads and railways	17.12%

Jewish land ownership outside the urban area of Jerusalem is quite insignificant. The Official Statistics of the Government of Palestine indicate that in 1946 the percentage of Jewish land ownership in the sub-district of Jerusalem did not exceed two per cent.[14]

Perils to Holy Places

Israel's domination and judaization of Jerusalem constitute a grave peril to the religious heritage of Christianity and Islam. Israel's threats against the *Haram Al-Sharif* and the desecrations of Christian and Islamic Holy Places were mentioned in Chapter 6. In this regard, it seems appropriate to refer to the report of the King-Crane Commission which prophetically warned of the danger to Christian and Moslem Holy Places were they to fall into Jewish hands. The King-Crane Commission was appointed in 1919 by the Supreme Council of the Allied Powers at the Paris Peace Conference to elucidate the state of opinion in Palestine and

Syria regarding the mode of settlement of their future following their detachment from Turkey. With respect to the Holy Places in Palestine, the Commission said:

> There is a further consideration that cannot be justly ignored, if the world is to look forward to Palestine becoming a definitely Jewish state, however gradually that may take place. That consideration grows out of the fact that Palestine is 'the Holy Land' for Jews, Christians, and Moslems alike. Millions of Christians and Moslems all over the world are quite as much concerned as the Jews with conditions in Palestine, especially with those conditions which touch upon religious feeling and rights. The relations in these matters in Palestine are most delicate and difficult. With the best possible intentions, it may be doubted whether the Jews could possibly seem to either Christians or Moslems proper guardians of the holy places, or custodians of the Holy Land as a whole. The reason is this: the places which are most sacred to Christians – those having to do with Jesus – and which are also sacred to Moslems, are not only not sacred to Jews, but abhorrent to them. It is simply impossible, under those circumstances, for Moslems and Christians to feel satisfied to have these places in Jewish hands, or under the custody of Jews. There are still other places about which Moslems must have the same feeling. In fact, from this point of view, the Moslems, just because the sacred places of all three religions are sacred to them, have made very naturally much more satisfactory custodians of the holy places than the Jews could be. It must be believed that the precise meaning, in this respect, of the complete Jewish occupation of Palestine has not been fully sensed by those who urge the extreme Zionist program. For it would intensify, with a certainty like fate, the anti-Jewish feeling both in Palestine and in all other portions of the world which look to Palestine as 'the Holy Land'.[15]

The fears expressed by the King-Crane Commission about the dangers involved in the Jewish domination of Palestine and its Holy Places, and confirmed by Israeli actions in Jerusalem, constitute a writing on the wall.

Notes

1. Cited in O. Kelly Ingram (ed.), *Jerusalem* (Triangle Friends of the Middle East, Durham NC, 1978), p. 26.

2. Translation from *Journal des Débats*, 30 March 1919, cited by Philippe de Saint Robert in *Le Jeu de la France en Méditerranée* (Julliard, Paris, 1970), p. 222.

3. M. Franco, *Histoire des Israélites de l'Empire Ottoman* (Durlacher, Paris, 1897), pp. 4, 5 and 195.

4. A.S. Rappoport, *Histoire de la Palestine* (Payot, Paris, 1932), p. 210.

5. C.M. Watson, *The Story of Jerusalem* (Dent, London, 1912), p. 278.

6. Ronald Storrs, *Orientations* (Nicholson and Watson, London, 1945), p. 280.

7. Official Records of the 2nd session of the General Assembly, Ad Hoc Committee on the Palestine Question, p. 304.

8. The sub-district of Jerusalem was the administrative unit which embraced the city, its suburbs and surrounding villages.

9. Official Records of the 2nd session, p. 292.

10. Government of Palestine, *Statistical Abstract 1944-1945*, pp. 36 and 46.

11. One *dunom* equals one thousand square metres.

12. UN Doc.1/A.14/32, p. 270, 11 November 1947.

13. Sami Hadawi, *Palestine, Loss of a Heritage* (Naylor, San Antonio, Texas), 1963, p. 141.

14. UN Doc.A/AC.14/32, p. 293.

15. J.C. Hurewitz, *Diplomacy in the Near and Middle East*, Vol. II (Van Nostrand, Princeton, 1956), p. 70. For a full report on the King-Crane Commission's investigation, see Harry N. Howard, *The King-Crane Commission* (Khayat, Beirut, 1963).

Chapter Nine

INTERNATIONAL LEGAL STATUS OF JERUSALEM

Status of Jerusalem in Turkish Times

Despite its religious and historic character, Jerusalem did not possess a distinctive status that differentiated it from other cities in Palestine until towards the end of the nineteenth century. On account of its international importance and a growing interest shown by Jews in emigrating to Palestine, Jerusalem and its surroundings were accorded an 'autonomous' and 'independent' status under the Turkish administrative reorganization of 1887-8. Such status did not involve any autonomy as its name may suggest but simply meant that Jerusalem ceased to be under the authority of the governor of the province and was linked to Constantinople, the capital of the Ottoman Empire.[1]

Status of Jerusalem After the Detachment of Palestine From Turkey

A radical change in the legal status of Jerusalem occurred at the end of the First World War when the Allied Powers decided to detach the Arab territories from the Ottoman Empire and to recognize independent Arab states in those territories. Article 22 of the Covenant of the League of Nations provided, as we have seen, that certain communities which formerly formed part of Turkey have reached a stage of development where their existence as independent nations can be provisionally recognized, subject to the rendering of administrative advice and assistance by a Mandatory, until such time as they are able to stand alone.

The effect of the recognition by Article 22 of the Covenant of the people of Palestine, amongst others, as an independent nation, taken in conjunction with Turkey's renunciation of its sovereignty by virtue of the Treaty of Lausanne (1923) over the Arab territories detached from it, was to make of Palestine a separate and independent international entity or, in other words, a state under international law. The personality of Palestine as a state was distinct and separate from the personality of the Mandatory. Although under the terms of the mandate granted by the League of Nations to Great Britain over Palestine, the

British Government exercised powers of legislation and administration (Article 1) and was entrusted with the control of the foreign relations of Palestine (Article 12), the State of Palestine retained its proper personality, concluded agreements with the Mandatory and, through its instrumentality, became party to a number of international treaties and conventions. The seat of the Government of Palestine was located in Jerusalem which thus became the capital of the State of Palestine. The direct consequence of these political and constitutional changes and developments was that Jerusalem passed from the sovereignty of Turkey to the sovereignty of the people of Palestine.

Status of Jerusalem Under Resolution 181 (II)

Another fundamental change occurred in the legal status of Jerusalem as a result of resolution 181 (II) which was adopted by the General Assembly on 29 November 1947. This resolution recommended, *inter alia*, the establishment of an international régime for Jerusalem. The resolution stated:

> The City of Jerusalem shall be established as a *corpus separatum* under a special international régime and shall be administered by the United Nations. The Trusteeship Council shall be designated to discharge the responsibilities of the Administering Authority on behalf of the United Nations.
> The City of Jerusalem shall include the present municipality of Jerusalem plus the surrounding villages and towns, the most eastern of which shall be Abu Dis; the most southern, Bethlehem; the most western, Ein Karem (including also the built-up area of Motsa); and the most northern Shu'fat, as indicated on the attached sketch-map (annex B).

The resolution laid down a Statute for the administration of the city. This Statute envisaged the appointment by the Trusteeship Council of a Governor to administer the city and conduct its external affairs, subject to the provision that existing local autonomous units in the territory of the city (villages, townships and municipalities) shall enjoy wide powers of local government and administration. The city would be demilitarized and its neutrality declared and preserved. A Legislative Council elected by the residents of the city would have powers of legislation and taxation. These provisions were to be elaborated and incorporated within five months in a detailed Statute of the city. Such Statute was to come into force not later than 1 October 1948 and was to remain in force in the first instance for a period of ten years, unless the Trusteeship Council finds it necessary to undertake a re-examination of these provisions at an earlier date. After the expiration of this period, the whole scheme shall be subject to re-examination by the Trusteeship Council in the light of the experience acquired with its functioning. The residents of the city shall be then free to express by means of a referendum their wishes as to possible modifications of the régime of the city.

The effect of resolution 181 (II) was, therefore, to clothe Jerusalem with an international legal status compatible with its historical character and its religious significance to the world.

Whether Status of Jerusalem was Affected by Subsequent Events

In view of subsequent developments which were not in line with the intentions and provisions of the resolution, it may be relevant to examine whether it was abrogated or its legal effect impaired by reason of the occupation and annexation of modern Jerusalem by Israel and of the Old City by Jordan, or by the subsequent occupation and annexation of the Old City by Israel in 1967.

The occupation and annexation of Jerusalem, whether by Israel or by Jordan, violated its legal status but did not abrogate resolution 181 (II) or impair its legal effect. In this regard, a distinction should be made between the provisions of the resolution that lay down the principle of the internationalization of the city, on the one hand, and those that concern its administration, on the other. Even though the provisions relative to the administration of the city were frustrated and their application thwarted by the military occupation of Jerusalem, the principle of internationalization itself remained unimpaired.

It is noteworthy that Hassan Bin Talal, the Crown Prince of Jordan, recently expressed the view that the Armistice Agreement concluded on 3 April 1949 between Israel and Jordan, and General Assembly resolutions 181 (II), 194 (III) and 303 (IV) precluded either Israel or Jordan from acquiring any title in respect of Jerusalem and, accordingly, the status of Jerusalem was not affected by the occupation of the city by those two states between 1948 and 1967. Crown Prince Hassan states:

The Armistice of April, 1949, precluded either State asserting or implementing any supposed title to territorial sovereignty in respect of Jerusalem. The U.N. resolution of 1949 had preserved the features of the Partition Resolution of November, 1947, relating to a special international régime for the City, even after the fighting had been concluded by the Armistice. A U.N. resolution adopted after the end of the fighting was inconsistent with any recognition by the international community of States of territorial sovereignty over Jerusalem, or any part of it, being accorded to any State. Such sovereignty remained in suspense pending the outcome of the proposals. An international imprint or status had been placed upon Jerusalem deriving from the original Partition Plan of 1947 and the later U.N. Resolutions of 1948 and 1949, which had not been vitiated, so far as Jerusalem was concerned, either by the fighting of 1948 or the *de facto* occupation and control of the two States in their respective areas of the City.[2]

The non-implementation or even the violation of a UN resolution does not entail its lapse or abrogation. There is no basis in legal theory for the lapse or abrogation of a resolution by reason of its non-implementation, just as there exists no basis for the abrogation or lapse of the various resolutions which have called for the repatriation of the Palestine refugees, or which have condemned and declared invalid the measures taken by Israel in Jerusalem, by reason of their non-implementation by Israel. Were it otherwise, it would mean that any UN resolution would be abrogated by its violation. Accordingly, the provisions of resolution 181 (II) for the establishment of a special international régime in Jerusalem continue to be valid and binding.

Israel is Bound by Resolution 181 (II)

It does not lie in Israel's power to argue that resolution 181 (II) possesses no obligatory force and is not binding on it for the simple reason that Israel itself derived its existence from the same resolution. Hence, by claiming that the resolution possesses no binding force, it would be tearing up its own birth certificate.

Moreover, Israel is also bound by resolution 181 (II) because of the undertakings it gave to the UN for its respect and observance.

A first undertaking to that effect was given by the cablegram dated 15 May 1948 addressed by M. Shertok, Foreign Secretary of the Provisional Government of Israel, to the Secretary-General of the UN. In this cablegram the Israeli Government expressed its readiness to co-operate with the UN 'in implementation of resolution of the General Assembly of 29 November 1947' and also 'to sign declaration and undertaking provided for respectively in part one C and part one D of resolution of General Assembly'.[3]

A second undertaking was given by Israel in 1949 in connection with its application for admission to UN membership. In fact, Israel was admitted to UN membership only after it gave formal assurances concerning its observance of General Assembly resolutions 181 (II) and 194 (III), including their provisions relating to Jerusalem. The debate at the General Assembly and the assurances then given by Israel were mentioned in Chapter 5. It is significant to observe that during this debate, Abba Eban, Israel's representative, recognized the legal status of Jerusalem as he emphasized that 'the legal status of Jerusalem is different from the territory in which Israel is sovereign'.[4]

Resolution 181 (II) is Not Binding on the Palestinians

The only party which is not bound by resolution 181 (II) is the Palestinians. The reason is that the Palestinians are the only people who possessed sovereignty over Palestine at the date on which the resolution was adopted. The question of the sovereignty of the Palestinians over Palestine, including Jerusalem, may perhaps require some elaboration.

In Turkish times, Arab and Turkish citizens enjoyed equal civil and political rights and hence shared sovereignty over all the territories – whether Turkish or Arab – of the Ottoman Empire. Upon the detachment of the Arab territories from Turkey and the creation of the five Arab States of Iraq, Lebanon, Palestine, Syria and Jordan at the end of the First World War, sovereignty over the territory of each of those five States vested in the inhabitants of each of those territories. Accordingly, sovereignty over Palestine vested in the people of Palestine whose existence as an independent nation was, moreover, recognized by Article 22 of the Covenant of the League of Nations. The mandate which was granted to Great Britain in 1922 to administer Palestine did not and could not divest the Palestinians of their right of sovereignty. This view is now recognized by all international jurists. The Palestinians were merely deprived of its exercise during the existence of the mandate which, in its inception and nature, was intended to be temporary until the people of Palestine would 'be able to stand alone'.[5] Hence, at all material times after the detachment of Palestine from Turkey, sovereignty over Palestine, including Jerusalem, belonged to the people of Palestine.

Resolution 181 (II) did not divest the Palestinians of their sovereignty over the City of Jerusalem. The fact that the resolution attributed to the Trusteeship Council the power to administer Jerusalem on behalf of the UN did not have the effect of vesting sovereignty over the city in the Trusteeship Council or in the UN. The power of administration of a territory and the right of sovereignty over such territory are two different things. Just as the British Government did not, according to the generally accepted opinion, acquire sovereignty over Palestine during the period of the mandate, though vested by the League of Nations with 'full powers of legislation and administration' (Article 1 of the mandate), similarly the giving to the Trusteeship Council of lesser powers, i.e. powers of administration only, but not of legislation, did not confer on it sovereignty over the City of Jerusalem. Powers of legislation and taxation were reserved by the resolution for the residents of the city who, it was envisaged, would exercise them through an elected Legislative Council.

Not only did resolution 181 (II) not divest the Palestinians of their sovereignty over Jerusalem, it could not do so even had it intended to achieve such a result. For one does not see how the UN could abrogate, impair or otherwise interfere with the vested rights and the sovereignty of the Palestinians, the original inhabitants of Palestine, over their country or any part of it. The sovereignty of the people of Palestine could not be extinguished by a resolution of the UN. Accordingly, there exists no escape from the conclusion that resolution 181 (II) did not deprive the people of Palestine of their sovereignty, nor bind the Palestinians, in the absence of their acceptance of its provisions.

Reaffirmation of Internationalization

The principle of the internationalization of the City of Jerusalem was reaffirmed, as we have seen, by the General Assembly in 1948 in resolution 194 (III) and again in 1949 in resolution 303 (IV). The significance of these reaffirmations lies principally in the fact that they were made *after* Israel's occupation of modern Jerusalem and Jordan's occupation of the Old City, thus making it clear that the General Assembly did not condone the occupation of the city or abandon its plan for its internationalization.

UN Invokes Legal Status of Jerusalem to Condemn Israel's Actions

In several resolutions adopted since 1967, the General Assembly and the Security Council have invoked the legal status of Jerusalem to condemn Israel's occupation and annexation of the Old City and to declare null and void all measures it has taken to change such status.

It is noteworthy that in these resolutions the UN refers to 'the status of Jerusalem', or to 'the legal status of Jerusalem' (Security Council resolution 252 of 21 May 1968 and General Assembly resolution 32/5 of 28 October 1977), or to 'the specific status of Jerusalem' (Security Council resolutions 452 of 20 July 1979, 465 of 1 March 1980 and 476 of 30 June 1980). The only 'status' or 'legal status' or 'specific status' which Jerusalem possesses is that laid down in resolution 181 (II) of 29 November 1947.

Moreover, some resolutions of the Security Council, namely 267 of 3 July 1969, 271 of 15 September 1969 and 298 of 25 September 1971, and General Assembly resolution 2253 of 4 July 1967, refer to the status of 'the City of Jerusalem'. The appellation 'City of Jerusalem' is derived from resolution 181 (II) and indicates the *corpus separatum* as defined by the General Assembly in 1947.

Such also is the view of the Committee on the Exercise of the Inalienable Rights of the Palestinians which was established by the General Assembly in its resolution 3376 (XXX) dated 10 November 1975. The Committee considers that the references to 'the status of Jerusalem' or 'the legal status of Jerusalem' in General Assembly and Security Council resolutions adopted following the occupation of the entire City of Jerusalem in June 1967 could mean only the status defined in the fundamental General Assembly resolution on the partition of Palestine, i.e. a *corpus separatum* under an international régime.[6]

The reliance by the UN on the status or the legal status of Jerusalem to invalidate the measures taken by Israel is significant in two respects.

On the one hand, such reliance amounts to an enforcement of the principle of the internationalization of Jerusalem. In other terms, though internationalization has not been implemented on the ground, yet its legal consequences are recognized and full effect is given to them in order to invalidate all measures taken in the city which are contrary to its status.

On the other hand, the enforcement of the legal consequences of internationalization must perforce apply to the modern section of Jerusalem which is an integral part of the *corpus separatum* as defined by resolution 181 (II). Both the Old City and modern Jerusalem enjoy the same legal status. No difference in fact or in law exists between them and it is not conceivable that one part should be treated differently from the other. The illegality of Israel's presence and actions in Jerusalem is indivisible since its international legal status encompasses its two sections, old and new.

Non-recognition of the Annexation of Jerusalem by the International Community

The condemnation of the annexation of Jerusalem, whether of its modern section or of the Old City, was not confined to resolutions of the UN. The principle of the internationalization of Jerusalem was also invoked by the community of nations which have refused to recognize its annexation, whether by Israel or by Jordan.

As regards Israel's occupation and subsequent annexation of modern Jerusalem, already in 1949 President Truman, whose efforts had largely brought Israel into existence, disapproved of its seizure of territories in excess of the boundaries specified for the Jewish State by resolution 181 (II) and considered Israel's disregard of the provisions of the resolution concerning partition, frontiers, refugees and internationalization of Jerusalem as dangerous to peace.[7]

When despite US disapproval, Israel took the first steps for the annexation of modern Jerusalem, the US Government refused to recognize the validity of Israel's actions and rejected Israel's request for the transfer of the American embassy from Tel-Aviv to Jerusalem which it had proclaimed to be its capital. Secretary of State Dulles then emphasized that Jerusalem is, above all, the holy place of the Christian, Moslem and Jewish faiths and that the world religious community has claims in Jerusalem which take precedence over the political claims of any particular nations.[8] The State Department declared:

> The Department of State was informed on July 10 by the Israeli Government that it intends to transfer its Foreign Ministry from Tel Aviv to Jerusalem as of July 12, 1953.
> The United States does not plan to transfer its Embassy from Tel Aviv to Jerusalem. It is felt that this would be inconsistent with the UN resolutions dealing with the international nature of Jerusalem...[9]

Secretary of State Dulles also stated that the UN has a primary responsibility for determining the future status of Jerusalem and that the presently standing UN resolution about Jerusalem contemplates that it should be, to a large extent at least, an international city rather than a purely national city.[10]

Most other states observed the same attitude as the US with respect to the non-recognition of the Israeli occupation and annexation of modern Jerusalem.

The same attitude of non-recognition was adopted by the community of nations with regard to the incorporation of the Old City of Jerusalem into the Hashemite Kingdom of Jordan. The only state to recognize Jordanian sovereignty over the Old City was Pakistan. All other states considered that Jordan, like Israel, exercised only *de facto* authority over the part of the city which they occupied.

Likewise, when Israel captured and annexed the Old City of Jerusalem in 1967, the community of nations disavowed Israel's actions. A statement then made by the UK Government reflects the international attitude in this regard. In a written reply to the House of Commons made on 27 November 1967, the British Foreign Office said:

> While Her Majesty's Government have, since 1949, recognized the *de facto* authority of Israel and Jordan in the parts of Jerusalem which they occupied, they, in common with many other governments, have not recognized *de jure* Israeli or Jordanian sovereignty over any part of the area defined in General Assembly resolution 303 (IV) of the 9th December 1949, which called for an international status for a designated area of Jerusalem.
>
> In the light of this United Nations resolution H.M. Government have held that the status of this area could be determined only in the context of a settlement in the Middle East.
>
> It would in present circumstances be inconsistent with this position to take any action, such as the recognition of Jerusalem as the capital of Israel, or the establishment of Her Majesty's Embassy there, which would imply recognition of Israel's sovereignty in West Jerusalem.

Similarly, the US Government reaffirmed its attitude of non-recognition of the annexation. It declared immediately after Israel's action:

> The United States have never recognized such unilateral actions by any of the States in the area as governing the international status of Jerusalem.[11]

At the Fifth Emergency Special Session of the General Assembly, US Ambassador Goldberg declared on 14 July 1967:

> With regard to the specific measures taken by the Government of Israel on 28 June, I wish to make it clear that the United States does not accept or recognize these measures as altering the status of Jerusalem.

Again, on 1 July 1969, US Ambassador Yost told the Security Council:

> Jerusalem is a sacred shrine to three of the world's largest and oldest religious faiths: Islam, Christianity and Judaism. By virtue of that fact, the United States has always considered that Jerusalem enjoys a unique international standing and that no action should be taken there without full regard to Jerusalem's special history and special place in the world community.

Like the US and the UK, most other nations refused to recognize Israel's annexation of Jerusalem, including its modern section, or to move their embassies from Tel-Aviv to Jerusalem. Only the Netherlands and twelve Latin American countries maintain at present their embassies in Jerusalem. These are: Costa Rica, Colombia, Bolivia, Chile, Dominican Republic, Ecuador, Salvador, Haiti, Panama, Uruguay, Guatemala and Venezuela. Save for those exceptions, the international community has generally disavowed the Israeli action in Jerusalem.

The non-recognition of the measures taken by Israel in Jerusalem was affirmed by several resolutions of the Conference of Islamic States. This Conference was formed in 1969 as a result of the arson committed at the Mosque of Al-Aqsa and it set up the Organization of the Islamic Conference. The latter Organization convenes annually at a conference of the Foreign Ministers of Islamic States.

At its meeting at Fez (8-12 May 1979) the Organization of the Islamic Conference which was attended by forty Arab and Islamic States emphasized the religious and spiritual importance of Jerusalem to all Moslems and considered that 'the liberation of *Al-Qods* [Jerusalem] from colonialist and racist Zionism, its restoration to Arab sovereignty and the preservation of its ancestral character, constitute a collective Islamic responsibility'. Of particular importance among the resolutions adopted by the Conference was resolution 3/10 which, *inter alia*,

- reaffirmed the commitment of all Member States to act for the liberation of Jerusalem and its restoration to Arab and Islamic sovereignty;
- affirmed the commitment of Member States to take adequate measures for the implementation of resolutions adopted by the UN with respect to Jerusalem since 1947; and
- asked all Member States to exhort all states which have embassies in Israel to resist Israeli pressures for their transfer to the Holy City of Jerusalem, in deference to the feelings of Moslems and in conformity with UN resolutions, pointing out the negative effects which the transfer of an embassy could have on relations with Islamic States.[12]

Again at its meeting at Islamabad on 29 January 1980, the Organization of the Islamic Conference invited the Islamic States 'to reaffirm their solidarity with the Arab States for the liberation of Jerusalem and all other occupied territories'.

It is relevant to mention also the Vatican's opposition to the annexation of Jerusalem. In his Encyclical *In Multiplicibus* of 24 October 1948 Pope Pius XII expressed the hope that 'an international régime, juridically established and guaranteed' should be applied to Jerusalem and its environs. The same hope was expressed by the Pope in his Encyclical *Redemptoria Nostri* dated 15 April 1949. Since then the Vatican has made several declarations which have advocated the adoption of a special statute for Jerusalem. More recently, in an address to the General Assembly of the UN on 2 October 1979, Pope John Paul II declared:

I also hope for a special statute that, under international guarantee – as my predecessor Paul VI indicated – would respect the particular nature of Jerusalem, a heritage sacred to the veneration of millions of believers of the three monotheistic religions, Judaism, Christianity and Islam.

It is not clear whether the 'special statute' which the Vatican advocates for Jerusalem represents an endorsement of the concept of the international régime recommended by the UN in 1947 or something else. What is perfectly clear, however, is that the Vatican's pronouncements amount to a rejection of Israel's annexation of the city.

Other Christian bodies have also expressed concern over the situation which prevails in Jerusalem. In July 1967 the National Council of

Churches went on record in favour of 'an international presence' in
Jerusalem and in December 1975 the General Assembly of the World
Council of Churches, at its meeting at Nairobi, declared that many
member churches are deeply concerned about the Christian Holy
Places and the Christian community of Jerusalem. The Council emphasized that the question of Jerusalem is not only a matter of protection
of the Holy Places: it is organically linked with living faiths and communities of people in the Holy City. Therefore, the General Assembly
deemed it essential 'that the Holy Shrines should not become mere
monuments of visitation but should serve as living places of worship
integrated and responsive to Christian communities who continue to
maintain their life and roots within the Holy City'.

Deviation by Egypt

Egypt is the only Arab country which has deviated from the almost
universal recognition of the international legal status of the City of
Jerusalem and from the worldwide condemnation of the Israeli annexation. This deviation occurred almost unperceived in the Egyptian-
Israeli peace negotiations and Peace Treaty of 26 March 1979.

In outlining his peace programme to the Knesset on 20 November
1977 during his spectacular but controversial visit to Jerusalem, President Anwar Sadat stated with regard to Jerusalem that he would insist,
as part of a peace settlement,

> on complete Israeli withdrawal from Arab Jerusalem, the city which
> was and will always be the living incarnation of the coexistence
> between the believers of the three revealed religions.
> It is unacceptable that anyone should think of the special position of
> Jerusalem in terms of annexation or expansion. Jerusalem should be
> a free city open to all believers.
> More important than all this, the city should not be cut away from
> those who have come to it during centuries. Rather than awaken
> hatreds of the kind of the Crusades, we should revive the spirit of
> Omar El Khattab and Saladin, in other words, the spirit of tolerance
> and respect of law.
> The places of worship, Islamic and Christian, are not meant only for
> the performance of religious rites. They bear testimony to our unin-
> terrupted political, spiritual and cultural presence in this city. No
> one should be mistaken about the importance that we, Christians and

Moslems, attach to Jerusalem and our veneration for it.

By confining his demand to an Israeli withdrawal from 'Arab Jerusalem', meaning presumably the Old City, President Sadat fell into the common error of imagining that only the Old City is Arab and that modern Jerusalem is Jewish. Moreover, by tacitly agreeing that modern Jerusalem can remain under Israel's dominion, he was acquiescing in its annexation by Israel and thus violating its international legal status.

The Camp David accords of 17 September 1978 did not face up to the question of Jerusalem. The parties were content to put on record their respective viewpoints in side letters addressed to President Carter under whose patronage the negotiations were held. In his letter to President Carter the Egyptian President set out Egypt's position that 'Arab Jerusalem' is an integral part of the West Bank and that it should be under Arab sovereignty. Israel's Prime Minister Begin wrote to President Carter that the Government of Israel had decided in July 1967 that Jerusalem is the capital of Israel. In a letter dated 22 September 1978 the US President informed President Sadat that the US position on Jerusalem remains as stated by Ambassador Goldberg in the General Assembly on 14 July 1967 and by Ambassador Yost in the Security Council on 1 July 1969. The purport of their statements which were noted above was that the US does not recognize the validity of the measures taken by Israel in Jerusalem since 1967.

Disagreement on the question of Jerusalem, however, did not prevent the conclusion of the Egyptian-Israeli Peace Treaty on 26 March 1979. It is significant to note that President Sadat signed the Treaty despite a formal declaration by Israel's Prime Minister a few days earlier in the Knesset that (a) Israel would not withdraw to its borders of 4 June 1967, (b) it would not allow the creation of a Palestinian State, and (c) that Jerusalem, one and unified, would remain for eternity the capital of Israel.

Although the Peace Treaty, like the Camp David accords, was silent about Jerusalem, it violated the status of Jerusalem. Article III of the Treaty stated that the parties 'recognize and will respect each other's sovereignty and territorial integrity and political independence'. In this regard one may ask: what sovereignty and what territorial integrity of Israel does Egypt thus recognize? Is it sovereignty over territory earmarked by resolution 181 (II) for the creation of a Jewish State against which Egypt voted at the UN? Or is it Israeli sovereignty over the territories which Israel seized in 1948 in excess of the same resolution comprising most of the area reserved for the Arab State as well as modern

Jerusalem and a large area of the *corpus separatum*? Or is it sovereignty over the Old City which it annexed in 1967? In Israel's estimation, its 'territorial integrity' includes all those territories. Strangely enough, Egypt's recognition of Israel's territorial integrity was even made without any reservation.

Despite the slipshod drafting of the Treaty which may explain the absence of any reservation that would limit Egypt's recognition of Israel's 'territorial integrity', Egypt did not recognize any rights in favour of Israel over the Old City. This has appeared clearly in the course of the 'autonomy' discussions that are being held between the parties. Egypt claimed that, under the Camp David accords, the Old City is part of the West Bank and hence its Arab inhabitants should be covered by the discussions concerning the 'autonomy' of the Palestinians while Israel, on the contrary, maintained that it has annexed the Old City which cannot, in its view, be subject to any negotiations. But even such an attitude on the part of Egypt does not excuse its action in recognizing Israel's 'territorial integrity' which violates the international legal status of Jerusalem.

It violates the status of modern Jerusalem since it amounts to an acquiescence in its annexation. Moreover, it also violates the status of the Old City because Egypt's claim that the Old City should be encompassed in the autonomy discussions ignores its international legal status and implies the abandonment of the benefit of the principles of international law which require the withdrawal of an aggressor, and also of the benefit of resolution 242 which called for Israel's withdrawal from territories recently occupied – a provision which indubitably includes the Old City. At best, the Egyptian position means the acceptance for the Old City of the Israeli plan which proposes to grant some kind of 'autonomy' to the Palestinians, a people that enjoyed sovereignty and full civil and political rights before Israel came into existence. The 'autonomy' plan is not a blessing for the Palestinians, as claimed by the authors of the Camp David accords, but a deceitful Israeli formula intended to disguise the continued Israeli occupation and colonization of Arab territories, including Jerusalem, and the continued subjection of the Palestinians to Israeli domination. Needless to observe that Egypt's deviation cannot affect the international legal status of Jerusalem.

Enforcement of the Internationalization of Jerusalem

It is perhaps necessary to emphasize that the recognition and enforcement of the international legal status of Jerusalem does not require the implementation of the machinery which was envisaged by resolution 181 (II) for the administration of the city. Such implementation is not appropriate by reason of the changes made by Israel since 1948 in the demographic composition of Jerusalem. These changes have resulted in a substantial diminution of its Christian and Moslem inhabitants, on the one hand, and the tripling of the number of its Jewish inhabitants, on the other hand, creating a ratio of one to four between Arabs and Jews. As a result of the demographic imbalance, the implementation of the international régime in the city under present conditions in accordance with resolution 181 (II) would, in effect, mean placing its administration and its future in the hands of the Jewish settlers brought by Israel for the express purpose of its judaization. In other words, the implementation of the resolution under present circumstances would lead, not to the internationalization of Jerusalem, but to its judaization. The principle of internationalization can be applied in a manner other than that envisaged by resolution 181 (II) and in a way which would be compatible with the rights and the sovereignty of the people of Palestine.

The inappropriateness of the implementation of the provisions for the administration of Jerusalem which were envisaged by resolution 181 (II) does not, however, imply the abandonment of the concept of internationalization which must continue to be respected and enforced since it is essential for the protection of Jerusalem and the preservation of its religious and historic character. In fact, as we have observed, the principle of internationalization was enforced by the UN in its condemnations and invalidations of Israeli actions in Jerusalem that violate its status. There remains to translate such condemnations and invalidations into facts and realities. Hence, the next step in the enforcement of the principle of internationalization must be the evacuation by Israel of the *corpus separatum* of Jerusalem and the effective rescission of the measures it has taken in violation of its status.

Notes

1. A. Heidelborn, *Droit Public et Administratif de L'Empire Ottoman* (Vienna-Leipzig, 1908), p. 7.

2. Hassan bin Talal, *A Study on Jerusalem* (Longman, London, 1979), pp. 25-6.

3. For text of cablegram, see Henry Cattan, *Palestine and International Law*, 2nd edn (Longman, London, 1976), p. 279.

4. Official Records of the 3rd Session of the General Assembly, Part II, Ad Hoc Political Committee, pp. 286-7, 1949.

5. On the question of sovereignty over Palestine during the British mandate,

see Cattan, *Palestine and International Law*, pp. 116-21.
    6. *The Status of Jerusalem* (United Nations, 1979), pp. 18, 20 and 26.
    7. James G. McDonald, *My Mission to Israel* (Simon and Schuster, New York, 1951), pp. 181-2.
    8. Department of State Bulletin, 15 June 1953, p. 832.
    9. Ibid., 20 July 1953, p. 82.
    10. Ibid., 10 August 1953, p. 177.
    11. Ibid., 28 June 1967, p. 57.
    12. It may be remarked that this provision received its first application in the summer of 1979 when, in execution of an election promise, the Canadian Government announced its intention to move its embassy in Israel from Tel-Aviv to Jerusalem but which it abandoned as a result of Arab and Islamic disapproval. In July 1980 a conference of the Islamic States held in Amman requested those countries that maintain their embassies in Jerusalem to move them out of the city and further warned of the severance of diplomatic and economic relations with such countries as maintain or establish embassies in Jerusalem.

Chapter Ten

NULLITY OF ISRAEL'S ACTIONS IN JERUSALEM

The measures taken by Israel in Jerusalem since 1948, whether with regard to annexation, or alteration of the demographic structure, or colonization, or dispossession of the Arab inhabitants and confiscation of their property, are null and void under international law and UN resolutions.

Nullity of Israel's Actions Under International Law

It is now a settled principle of the law of nations that no territory can be acquired by force or by war and that military occupation gives no title to the occupant. In the past, conquest, if successfully maintained, constituted a source of title. But since the end of the nineteenth century, the rule that no territory can be acquired by force or by war has become a principle of international law and has been implicitly affirmed by the Covenant of the League of Nations and the Charter of the United Nations.

It follows that Israel's occupation and annexation of Jerusalem, whether in 1948 or in 1967, were unlawful acts which gave it no right, title or sovereignty. Its status under international law is that of a belligerent occupier who exercises a *de facto* power only and whose conquest does not displace the sovereignty of the conquered. Neither the recognition of the aggressor by other states, nor passage of time, constitute a cure for the illegality of the occupation or the annexation.

Likewise, the alteration of the demographic structure of Jerusalem by means of the displacement of its original inhabitants, the refusal to allow their return and their replacement by Jewish settlers and immigrants is a barbaric action which violates international law.

So also the colonization of Jerusalem and the expropriation or confiscation of Arab property, whether of the refugees or of residents, are unlawful acts under international law and are consequently null and void. The rule is stated by Oppenheim as follows:

Immovable private enemy property may under no circumstances or conditions be appropriated by an invading belligerent. Should he confiscate and sell private land or buildings, the buyer would acquire no right whatever to the property.[1]

Oppenheim further observes that if the occupier has appropriated and sold private or public property which may not legitimately be appropriated by a military occupant, such property may afterwards be claimed from the purchaser without payment of compensation.[2] The same rule is expressed by D. P. O'Connell in these terms:

> As a result of treaty stipulations a customary rule of law has of now developed prohibiting the confiscations of private property in territory occupied by a belligerent. The most that the belligerent may do is sequestrate it, and it must be returned to the private owner when the belligerent occupation terminates.[3]

Nullity of Israel's Actions Under UN Resolutions

Israel's occupation and annexation of modern Jerusalem in 1948 and of the Old City in 1967 violated General Assembly resolutions 181 (II), 194 (III) and 303 (IV) and the international legal status established for the City of Jerusalem by these resolutions. Israel's occupation and annexation of Jerusalem constituted, therefore, an aggression on, and a usurpation of, an internationalized territory.

Israel's refusal to permit the repatriation of the Palestine refugees violated a long line of UN resolutions adopted since December 1948. Moreover, the UN has proclaimed in several resolutions adopted since 1967 that the measures taken by Israel to change the demographic structure of the occupied territories, including Jerusalem, have no legal validity and that Israel's policy of settling parts of its population and new immigrants in those territories constitutes a flagrant violation of the Fourth Geneva Convention Relative to the Protection of Civilian Persons in Time of War.

As regards refugee property, the General Assembly laid down in resolution 194 (III) the principle of restitution to the Palestine refugees in general of their homes. The restitution of other property owned by the refugees is implied. Then in resolution 394 (V) of 14 December 1950 the General Assembly directed the Conciliation Commission 'to continue negotiations with the parties concerned regarding measures for the protection of the rights, property and interests of the refugees'. Needless to say that the efforts of the Conciliation Commission to secure the abrogation by Israel of its confiscatory legislation of Arab refugee property proved to be fruitless and futile.

The nullity of the dispossession of the Palestinians and the confiscation of their property was further emphasized by General Assembly resolution 3236 (XXIX) of 22 November 1974 which 'reaffirmed the inalienable right of the Palestinians to return to their homes and property from which they have been displaced and uprooted'.

The principal resolutions of the General Assembly, the Security Council and the Commission on Human Rights which have condemned Israel's actions in Jerusalem since 1967 and declared their nullity are summarized hereinafter.

Condemnations by General Assembly

On 4 July 1967 the General Assembly adopted by a vote of 99 to nil, with 20 abstentions (including the US), resolution 2253(ES-V) in which it expressed concern at the measures taken by Israel to change the status of Jerusalem, declared these measures to be invalid, and called upon Israel to rescind them and to desist forthwith from taking any action which would alter the status of the city.

Then on 14 July 1967 the General Assembly adopted resolution 2254(ES-V) which deplored Israel's failure to implement its resolution of 4 July and reiterated its call on Israel to rescind measures taken and to desist from taking any action which would alter the status of Jerusalem.

Other resolutions of the General Assembly condemned the measures taken by Israel in the occupied territories, including Jerusalem, declared them to be completely null and void, and called for their rescission. Mention may be made, *inter alia*, of resolution 2851 (XXVI) of 20 December 1971, resolution 2949 (XXVII) of 8 December 1972, resolution 3005 (XXVII) of 15 December 1972, resolution 3092 (XXVIII) of 7 December 1973, resolution 3236 (XXIX) of 22 November 1974, resolution 3240 (XXIX) of 29 November 1974, resolution 3525 (XXX) of 15 December 1975, resolution 31/106 of 16 December 1976, resolution 32/5 of 28 October 1977, resolution 32/91 of 13 December 1977, resolution 33/113 of 18 December 1978 and resolution 34/70 of 6 December 1979.

Condemnations by Security Council

The Security Council adopted several resolutions, some of which dealt with the Arab-Israeli conflict generally, while others dealt specifically with the situation in Jerusalem.

Among the former the most important was resolution 242 of 22 November 1967. The provisions of this resolution apply to the Old City of Jerusalem in so far as they call for the withdrawal of Israeli armed forces 'from territories occupied in the recent conflict'.

Turning to the resolutions of the Security Council which dealt with Jerusalem specifically, mention may be made of the following:

Resolution 252 adopted on 21 May 1968 in which the Security Council declared that all legislative and administrative measures and actions taken by Israel, including expropriation of land and properties, which tend to change the legal status of Jerusalem, were invalid and could not change that status. The resolution called on Israel to rescind all such measures already taken and to desist forthwith from taking any further action which tends to change the status of Jerusalem. The Council requested the Secretary-General to report on the implementation of the resolution. In due course the Secretary-General reported that the Israeli Government's position in the matter remained unchanged (S/9149).

Resolution 267 adopted on 3 July 1969 in which the Security Council censured all measures taken to change the status of the City of Jerusalem, confirmed that all legislative and administrative measures and actions taken by Israel which purport to alter the status of Jerusalem, including expropriation of land and properties thereon, were invalid and urgently called once more upon Israel to rescind forthwith all measures taken which tend to change the status of the City of Jerusalem and to refrain from all actions likely to have such effect. Israel again ignored this resolution.

Resolution 271 adopted by the Security Council on 15 September 1968 following the arson perpetrated at the Mosque of Al-Aqsa in which it recognized that any act of destruction or profanation of the Holy Places, or any encouragement of, or connivance at, any such act might seriously endanger international peace and security. The Security Council declared that the execrable act of desecration and profanation of the Holy Mosque of Al-Aqsa emphasized the immediate necessity of Israel's desisting from acting in violation of UN resolutions and rescinding forthwith all measures and actions taken by it designed to alter the status of Jerusalem, and called upon Israel scrupulously to observe the provisions of the Geneva Convention and international law governing military occupation.

Resolution 298 adopted by the Security Council on 25 September 1971 which deplored Israel's failure to respect the previous resolutions adopted by the UN concerning measures and actions which purport to affect the status of the City of Jerusalem and declared that it confirms in the clearest possible terms that all legislative and administrative actions taken by Israel to change the status of the City of Jerusalem, including expropriations of land and properties, transfer of populations and legislation aimed at the incorporation of the occupied section are totally invalid and cannot change that status.

Resolution 446 adopted by the Security Council on 22 March 1979 which strongly deplored Israel's failure to abide by its resolutions and those of the General Assembly, called upon it to rescind the measures it has taken in the occupied territories, including Jerusalem, and established a Commission to examine and report on the situation relating to settlements in the occupied territories, including Jerusalem.

Resolution 452 adopted by the Security Council on 20 July 1979 in which it reconfirmed pertinent resolutions of the Council concerning Jerusalem and, in particular, the need to protect and preserve the unique spiritual and religious dimension of the Holy Places in that city.

Resolution 465 adopted by the Security Council on 1 March 1980 which condemned Israeli settlements in the occupied territories, including Jerusalem. This resolution was discussed in Chapter 7.

Resolution 476 adopted by the Security Council on 30 June 1980 which deplored the persistence of Israel in changing the physical character, demographic composition and institutional structure of the Holy City of Jerusalem and reiterated that all such measures which have altered the geographic, demographic and historical character and status of the Holy City of Jerusalem are null and void and must be rescinded in compliance with the relevant resolutions of the Security Council.

Condemnations by Commission on Human Rights

The Commission on Human Rights has also condemned Israel's violations of human rights and fundamental freedoms in the occupied territories, including Jerusalem. In its resolutions of 22 March 1972, 14 March 1973, 11 February 1974, 21 February 1975, 15 February 1977 and 21 February 1979 the Commission expressed its alarm and concern over Israel's implementation of massive programmes of immigration, its refusal to allow the return of the refugees, the destruction of houses, the expropriation of Arab properties, the ill-treatment of prisoners and the pillaging of the archaeological and cultural heritage in the occupied territories, including Jerusalem.

Nullity Extends to Israel's Actions in Modern Jerusalem

The nullity applies to all Israel's actions, whether in modern Jerusalem or in the Old City, regardless of whether they have occurred before or after 1967. The legal position is identical in all cases. Such nullity arises from the illegality of Israel's actions under international law and UN resolutions as well as from their violation of the international legal status of the city which comprises its two sections.[4] UN resolutions, and in particular Security Council resolutions 267 of 3 July 1969 and 298 of 25 September 1971, leave no doubt in this regard.

Notes

1. Oppenheim, *International Law*, 7th edn, Vol. 2 (Longman, London, 1952), p. 403.
2. Ibid., p. 619.
3. D.P. O'Connell, *International Law*, Vol. II (Stevens, London, 1970), p. 770.
4. In an analysis of UN resolutions, W.T. Mallison and S.V. Mallison reach the same conclusion, namely that UN resolutions adopted since 1967 which invalidate Israel's actions in Jerusalem apply to Israel's actions before 1967: *An International Analysis of the Major United Nations Resolutions Concerning the Palestine Question* (United Nations, 1979), pp. 51-4.

Chapter Eleven

WHETHER RESOLUTION 242 OR PARTITION OFFERS A SATISFACTORY SOLUTION

Resolution 242

Since resolution 242 still remains the target of diplomatic efforts for the settlement of the Arab-Israeli conflict, despite previous failures in that regard, it is pertinent to examine whether its implementation would offer a satisfactory solution of the problem of Jerusalem.

Applied to Jerusalem, the provisions of resolution 242 require Israel to withdraw its forces from territories occupied in the recent conflict. This means that Israel is required to withdraw from the Old City and adjacent areas of Jerusalem which it seized in June 1967. Israel's claim that it is not required to withdraw from all ocupied territories is untenable, not only because the resolution is abundantly clear both in its English and French texts in this respect, but also because the principle of the inadmissibility of the acquisition of territory by war laid down by the resolution applies to all territories without exception.

The resolution, however, is silent about withdrawal from modern Jerusalem and other areas of the *corpus separatum* which Israel seized in 1948. In this respect, therefore, the resolution is deficient and inadequate for the solution of the problem of Jerusalem. The silence of the resolution over Israel's withdrawal from modern Jerusalem might have been excused if it merely aimed at liquidating the territorial consequences of the war of 5 June 1967. This, however, does not appear to have been the case. The Security Council was more ambitious for it sought, according to the terms of the resolution, 'to work for a just and lasting peace' in the Middle East. To this end it proposed a package deal whereby Israel would withdraw from territories it occupied in 1967 in return for its recognition by the Arab States. It does not need much ingenuity to conclude that this formula would have the effect of shelving both the Palestine question and the problem of Jerusalem.

It is obvious that the Security Council cannot achieve its objective of working for a just and lasting peace by bypassing the core of the conflict, namely the Palestine question, and brushing it off as 'a refugee problem'. Similarly, it cannot solve the problem of Jerusalem by passing over Israel's usurpation of modern Jerusalem. It seems that the Security Council was more concerned in restoring the *fait accompli* of

1948 rather than in restoring right and justice.

The effect of resolution 242 was, therefore, to disavow Israel's aggression in one part of Jerusalem and to condone it in another part. Hence, it cannot be supported because the occupation and annexation of modern Jerusalem in 1948 and of the Old City in 1967 were both acts of aggression against the *corpus separatum* which violated international law and UN resolutions. There exists no difference between them. Both are equally unlawful and devoid of any legal effect and Israel is obligated to withdraw from the entirety of the *corpus separatum* of Jerusalem. The recognition of any territorial or sovereign rights in favour of Israel over any part of Jerusalem in consequence of such unlawful acts amounts to rewarding aggression and condoning the grave wrong done to the historic character of the city and its inhabitants.

The Security Council's failure in resolution 242 to insist upon Israel's withdrawal from modern Jerusalem, in addition to the Old City, cannot be construed as implying a tacit ratification of Israel's usurpation. The reason being that the Security Council does not possess the power to override the resolutions of the General Assembly which laid down an international legal status for the whole city. Although it is within the authority of the Security Council to interpret its own resolutions, it is beyond its power to impose limitations on the meaning or the scope of General Assembly resolutions.[1] Neither does it possess the power to ratify Israel's annexation and usurpation of part of the city or to make lawful what is unlawful. The Security Council has recognized and enforced the international legal status of the City of Jerusalem, as we have seen in Chapters 9 and 10, by proclaiming the nullity of the measures taken to change its legal status and it would lack coherence if its resolution 242 were to be construed as tantamount to a ratification of the annexation of modern Jerusalem.

There exist other imperative considerations that require Israel's evacuation of modern Jerusalem.

The first concerns the religious significance of modern Jerusalem to Christians and Moslems. While the Jews possess no Holy Places in modern Jerusalem outside the city walls, except some cemeteries in the eastern vicinity of Jerusalem, Christians and Moslems possess a large number of Holy Places, religious shrines and sanctuaries outside the Old City, some being located in modern Jerusalem, others in its vicinity. These Holy Places, mostly Christian, include the Cenacle, the Tomb of the Virgin, the Garden of Gethsemane, the Garden Tomb, the Mount of Olives, the Sanctuary of the Ascension and a number of churches, all located outside the Old City proper. The Christians also possess Holy

Places in the vicinity of Jerusalem as in Bethany, Bethlehem (Church of the Nativity, the Milk Grotto and Shepherds Field) and Ein Karem (birthplace of John the Baptist). The historic Moslem cemetery of Mamillah is located in modern Jerusalem. All these Holy Places, religious sites and churches are located in the area of the *corpus separatum* of Jerusalem as defined by the General Assembly in 1947.

The second consideration concerns the fifty to sixty thousand or more Christians and Moslems (now over one hundred thousand by reason of natural growth) who were displaced from their homes in 1948. In fact, most of the Arab population of Jerusalem, which was displaced in 1948, lived in modern Jerusalem. Roughly speaking, one-third of the Arab population lived in the Old City and two-thirds in modern Jerusalem. It is clear then that if Israel were allowed to remain permanently in control of modern Jerusalem, the majority of the Christian and Moslem population of Jerusalem would be condemned to perpetual exile from their homes and Jerusalem would lose its Arab and Christian character.

Partition of Jerusalem

The foregoing criticism of resolution 242 for its silence over Israel's withdrawal from modern Jerusalem applies equally to the proposal made in certain quarters for the partition of Jerusalem between Arabs and Jews whereby the latter would retain modern Jerusalem while the former would recover the Old City only.

Originally, the idea of the partition of Jerusalem was proposed in 1947 by the Jews to the UN during the General Assembly's debate on the question of Palestine. Addressing the Ad Hoc Committee on the Palestinian Question as the representative of the Jewish Agency, Dr Silver then 'strongly urged that the Jewish section of modern Jerusalem, outside the walls, should be included in the Jewish State'.[2] It is noteworthy that the Jewish claim was then limited to 'the Jewish section of modern Jerusalem' and did not extend to the whole of modern Jerusalem.

After the battle of Jerusalem in 1948 King Abdullah of Jordan, contrary to the attitude of the other Arab States, came to share the Jewish idea of the partition of Jerusalem and for this reason, like the Jews, he opposed the internationalization of the city. But he insisted in secret negotiations with Israel on its withdrawal from the Arab quarters of modern Jerusalem which Jewish forces had seized in 1948.

'Jordan', states H. Eugene Bovis, 'was deeply involved in secret negotiations with Israel for a settlement that would include division of Jerusalem between the two. Abdullah was asking Israel to cede the Jerusalem-Bethlehem road and the former Arab quarters of West Jerusalem. Israel was offering to make these concessions in exchange for the Jewish quarter of the Walled City.'[3] The assassination of King Abdullah put an end to these secret negotiations.

The idea of the partition of Jerusalem revived after the adoption of resolution 242. Some Arab statesmen saw in its provision for Israel's withdrawal from territories occupied in 1967 a means to restore under Arab rule the Old City and the Islamic Holy Places which it contains. In their enthusiasm to recover the Old City, the partisans of partition came to describe it as 'Arab Jerusalem', forgetting or possibly ignoring that modern Jerusalem contained a number of Arab quarters in which lived the majority of the Arab population of Jerusalem. This was a misconception which arose from the appellation after the war of 1948 of modern Jerusalem as the 'Jewish sector' and the Old City as the 'Arab sector', these being appellations that reflected the military picture as fixed by the Armistice Agreement between Israel and Jordan but which did not correspond to any historical or demographic division of the city. The same may be said of such new appellations as 'East Jerusalem' and 'West Jerusalem'.

In fact, Jerusalem was completely and almost exclusively Arab for eighteen hundred years. A Jewish quarter which was inhabited by a small number of religious Jews existed in the Old City. In the latter half of the nineteenth century, as a result of the growth of the population, some Jewish and Arab quarters were established outside the walls of the city. The first Jewish quarter outside the Old City – Montefiore, also known as Yamin Moshe – was established in 1862. This was followed by Measharim in 1875, Beth Israel in 1885 and the Bukhari Quarter in 1892. All the other Jewish quarters around Jerusalem that existed in 1948 were established during the British mandate.

As to the Arab quarters in modern Jerusalem, several of them were established in the latter half of the nineteenth century. The Arab quarters that existed in modern Jerusalem in 1948 were fifteen in number and were called: Bab El Zahreh, Sheikh Jarrah, Wadi Joz, Greek Colony, German Colony, Musrarah, Nebi Daoud, Mamillah, Deir Abu Tor, Upper Bakaa, Lower Bakaa, Ratisbonne, Talbieh, Katamon and Sheikh Bader. Only the first three remained in Arab hands in 1948 (and then only until 1967), while the twelve others were seized by Israel.

Modern Jerusalem, therefore, comprised in 1948 both Arab and Jewish quarters and had a mixed population of Arabs and Jews. As we have seen in Chapter 8, the Jews owned about one-quarter of modern Jerusalem. Hence to call modern Jerusalem 'Jewish Jerusalem' shows a total ignorance of the facts.

Finally, the partition of Jerusalem would gravely prejudice the Palestine question generally. By recognizing that Israel has acquired title and sovereignty over modern Jerusalem, the partisans of partition would thereby concede that Israel has also acquired title and sovereignty over the territories destined for the Arab State under resolution 181 (II) which it seized in 1948 in excess and in violation of the boundaries fixed by the resolution.

It is clear then that neither resolution 242 nor partition offers a just and lasting solution for the problem of Jerusalem.

Notes

1. W.T. Mallison and S.V. Mallison, *An International Analysis of the Major United Nations Resolutions Concerning the Palestine Question* (United Nations, 1979), p. 53.

2. Official Records of the 2nd Session of the General Assembly, Ad Hoc Committee on the Palestinian Question, 1947, p. 16.

3. H. Eugene Bovis, *The Jerusalem Question, 1917-1968* (Hoover Institute Press, Stanford, California, 1971), p. 74.

Chapter Twelve

OBSTACLES TO A SOLUTION

Israel's Obduracy

The first obstacle to a settlement of the problem of Jerusalem lies in the obduracy of Israel and its dogged determination to keep and judaize the city, regardless of its status or world opinion.

It is evident that one cannot secure by persuasion, negotiation or mere adoption of UN resolutions Israel's respect for the legal status of Jerusalem and the rescission of the measures it has taken in the city. Israel is determined to resist any change in Jerusalem and to hold it by force of arms, regardless of the rights of the original inhabitants it has displaced, regardless of principles of law and justice and regardless of world opinion and UN resolutions. It considers that the facts it has created in Jerusalem are irreversible. It has proclaimed that the 'integration' of Jerusalem in its territory is 'irrevocable' and 'not negotiable'.[1] In these circumstances, does it stand to reason that Israel will admit that it has illegally annexed Jerusalem and that it must withdraw from it? Is it realistic to assume that after having established a most amazing record of defiance of UN resolutions, Israel will graciously bow down, recognize its past errors and rescind the measures it has taken? Is it reasonable to expect that it will allow the Palestinian refugees to return to their homes, withdraw the settlers it has brought in and annul the confiscations of Arab property? It is completely utopian to imagine that Israel would redress the wrongs it has done by any means short of recourse to sanctions or the use of force.

US Support

The second obstacle to a settlement lies in the support which the US extends to Israel and its apparent acquiescence in Israel's actions. Israel's determination to resist any redress of the situation is considerably strengthened by the massive military and financial aid, and the political support, it receives from the US Government.

The US Government's policy with respect to Jerusalem has radically altered since 1947. The concern which the US Government had then shown for the future of Jerusalem and the protection of the Holy Places had abated with time. This is apparent from an examination of the manner in which the US Government has voted at the UN since the 1960s on the illegal behaviour of Israel at Jerusalem. Although on certain occasions the US has joined other nations in condemning Israel's actions,[2] yet on others it acted in a manner that was not conducive to the restoration of legality and justice. On many occasions it abstained from, or voted against, resolutions that censured or condemned Israel for its actions in Jerusalem.

Thus at the Fifth Emergency Special Session of the General Assembly which convened on 17 June 1967 to consider the situation arising from Israel's occupation of the West Bank, including Jerusalem, Gaza, Sinai and the Golan, the US, contrary to the attitude it observed in 1956 regarding the Suez War, opposed Israel's condemnation as an aggressor as it also opposed the adoption of a resolution calling for its immediate and unconditional withdrawal. Instead, it proposed a resolution which, in effect, aimed at the extraction from the victims of the aggression of political gains in favour of Israel as a price for its withdrawal, an objective which it achieved in resolution 242. However, even this did not satisfy Israel, because it wanted both territory and political gains with the result that no withdrawal has taken place since 1967 and Israel has continued until today to occupy Arab territories, including Jerusalem.

The political support which the US Government has extended to Israel since then is evident from the attitude it has adopted in regard to UN resolutions that questioned or condemned or censured Israel's conduct in the occupied territories, including Jerusalem. The US Government *abstained* from General Assembly resolutions 2253 and 2254 of 4 and 14 July 1967 which called upon Israel to rescind the measures it had taken to alter the status of Jerusalem. It *voted against* General Assembly resolution 2851 (XXVI) of 20 December 1971 which declared that all measures taken by Israel to settle the occupied territories, including Jerusalem, are completely null and void. It *voted against* resolution 3005 (XXVII) dated 15 December 1972 which declared that all measures taken by Israel in contravention of the Geneva Convention of 12 August 1949 to settle the occupied territories, including Jerusalem, are null and void. It *abstained* from supporting General Assembly resolution 32/5 dated 28 October 1977 which deplored the persistence of Israel in establishing settlements and called upon it to desist from changing the legal status, geographical nature or demographic composition of the Arab territories occupied since 1967, including Jerusalem. It *voted against* General Assembly resolution 33/113 (c) dated 18 December 1978 which reaffirmed the nullity of the measures taken by Israel in Jerusalem. It *abstained* from Security Council resolution 446 of 22 March 1979 which called upon Israel to rescind the measures it has taken to change the legal status, geographical nature and demographic composition of Arab territories, including Jerusalem. The extraordinary disavowal by President Carter of the US vote on 1 March 1980 in favour of Security Council resolution 465 which condemned Israeli settlements and called for their dismantlement seems to suggest an acquiescence in Israel's unlawful colonization of Jerusalem, or possibly a conflict of views on the matter between the State Department and the White House. It *abstained* from Security Council resolution 476 of 30 June 1980 which deplored the persistence of Israel in changing the physical character, demographic composition, institutional structure and the status of the Holy City of Jerusalem and proclaimed the nullity and legal invalidity of the measures taken by Israel in this regard.

The voting history of the US Government at the UN regarding Jerusalem has been the subject of sharp criticism:

> The United Nations has been demonstrably unable to induce Israel to halt her annexation of East Jerusalem. The United Nations failure in this respect was ascribed by some observers to the absence of wholehearted support by the United States. In fact, Washington's policies toward Jerusalem were viewed by some critics as incompatible with its sponsorship of the principle of military withdrawal contained in the November 1967 United Nations resolution and as lacking sincerity and consistency.[3]

Despite the US Government's protestations of innocence and its numerous statements declaring that it does not sanction the measures taken by Israel in Jerusalem, it seems fair to suggest that its refusal in June 1967 to join other nations in pressing for an Israeli withdrawal coupled to its veto of, and abstention on, UN resolutions condemning Israel's unlawful actions has encouraged Israel to annex the Old City and to implant itself more deeply in it by a massive colonization programme.

The support which the US Government extends to Israel is greatly enhanced by its proclaimed opposition to the recourse by the UN to sanctions against Israel. The US Government is unwilling to withhold aid from Israel as a means of pressure to secure its withdrawal from Jerusalem or other territories occupied in 1967. This was emphasized by President Carter at a news conference on 23 August 1977 when he said that although the territory Israel occupied in 1967 'was not part of

Israel', he had no intention to exert pressure on it by cutting off economic and military aid in order to secure its withdrawal from such territory. This can only mean that Israel has the US blessing to continue indefinitely in occupation and in the judaization of the Holy City and other Arab territories despite the condemnation of those acts by world opinion.

This is all the more regrettable when it is realized that the only cases where Israel was forced to abandon unlawful activities were the result of US pressure: the suspension by the US Government of Mutual Assistance funds to Israel in September 1953 succeeded in securing the stoppage of the drainage work undertaken by it in the Syrian-Israeli Demilitarized Zone in contempt of the UN; the strong condemnation by President Eisenhower of the Suez aggression in 1956 and his threat to suspend public assistance to Israel and to eliminate the tax credits allowed on private contributions to Israel were instrumental in securing its withdrawal from the territories it had then occupied; the threat made by the US Government in March 1975, following Henry Kissinger's failure to secure a partial Israeli withdrawal from Sinai, that it would undertake a 'reappraisal' of its policy in the Middle East coupled to the deferment of arms deliveries quickly led to Israel's acceptance of a partial withdrawal from Sinai.

It is clear then that in the absence of a reversal by the US of its policy with respect to Jerusalem, there seems to be no hope of a peaceful solution.

Notes

1. UN Docs.A/6793 and S/8146, 12 September 1967.
2. E.g. in Security Council resolutions 252 dated 21 May 1968, 267 dated 3 July 1969, 271 dated 15 September 1969 and 298 dated 25 September 1971.
3. Richard H. Pfaff, *Jerusalem: Keystone of an Arab-Israeli Settlement* (American Enterprise Institute for Public Policy Research, Washington DC, 1969), p. 44.

Chapter Thirteen

CONSERVATORY MEASURES PENDING
FINAL SETTLEMENT

The Future

What does the future hold in store for Jerusalem? Sometimes one can read the future by scrutinizing the past. If we look back at the troubled history of Jerusalem over the ages, we find in the Latin Kingdom of Jerusalem a close parallel to the régime which now dominates the Holy City. The Latin Kingdom possessed the same characteristics as we actually find in Israel. It was forcibly established by an alien people on an Arab land amidst a hostile Arab world and was structured on race and religion. One basic difference, however, exists between them: unlike Israel, the Latin Kingdom did not uproot the native inhabitants from their homes or dispossess them of their lands.

The Latin Kingdom lasted in Jerusalem from 1099 until 1187, a period of eighty-eight years, and then collapsed at the point of the sword. The lesson to be drawn from its rise and fall is the handwriting on the wall. If Israel persists in its obduracy in refusing redress of the wrongs it has done, it might well suffer the same fate.

One would hope that the problem of Jerusalem should not, as in the case of the Latin Kingdom, have to be settled by the sword. In the twentieth century there exists, at least on the statute book, international legal machinery for the settlement of disputes and the redress of national wrongs. The Charter, the UN, the International Court of Justice were established after the terrible holocaust of the Second World War specifically in order to correct grave injustices and preserve peace among nations. Unfortunately, in the Palestine Question, including the problem of Jerusalem, the principles of the Charter were trampled upon,[1] the resolutions of the UN flouted,[2] and recourse to the International Court of Justice thwarted.[3] Moreover, it has not been possible until now for the Security Council to impose sanctions upon Israel to force it to comply with UN resolutions because of the standing US veto against the imposition of sanctions on Israel. All avenues for redress being thus closed, the conditions seem to be present to make war the only alternative available for correcting the situation. History, in fact, teaches us that some national wrongs and certain situations cannot be corrected, save by recourse to force. So long as the Israelis do

143

not recognize the gross injustices they have committed in Palestine and show no willingness to redress the wrongs done, of which there exists no sign whatsoever, it is futile to imagine that the Palestine Question and the problem of Jerusalem can be peaceably resolved.

Need to Preserve Jerusalem

This being the case, should the world allow the situation to deteriorate further and further until it explodes? There are cogent reasons for the taking of immediate action to save Jerusalem, even though a settlement of the problem is not in the offing. First, Israel is transforming Jerusalem, physically and demographically, by leaps and bounds and in defiance of UN resolutions and world disapproval. Its intention is clearly to create what it imagines will be irreversible facts. Second, its presence and domination of the city constitute a source of great danger. One more grave desecration of its Holy Places – like the arson at the Mosque of Al-Aqsa – could spark off a war, if not a world conflagration. All three Arab-Israeli armed conflicts of 1956, 1967 and 1973 came very near to bringing about superpower confrontations. Third, Israel's occupation and annexation of Jerusalem, and the measures it has taken for its judaization, constitute flagrant violations of international law and UN resolutions. The prolongation of its presence in Jerusalem works to its advantage as aggressor by enabling it to colonize it on a massive scale and to alter profoundly its historic character. A military occupier possesses no right to take measures such as annexation, transfer of population, confiscation of property, settlement of immigrants and alteration of the physical and demographic features of an occupied city. Not one of those actions can be defended.

Conservatory Measures

The UN may not be competent to impose a settlement of the Arab-Israeli conflict, but it is fully competent and even duty bound to take, in implementation of its resolutions and pending a final settlement, all conservatory or protective measures intended to arrest the process of the judaization of Jerusalem, to rescind Israel's unlawful actions which violate its status, and to preserve the religious and historic heritage of the world in the Holy City.

The taking of such conservatory measures is further dictated by the obligation of the UN to honour the guarantee which it assumed in 1947 with regard to Holy Places, religious and minority rights. Resolution 181 (II) provided in Part I C that its provisions with respect to Holy Places and religious and minority rights shall be embodied in a declaration to be made to the UN by the Provisional Governments of the Arab and Jewish States. The Provisional Government of Israel assumed its obligations in this regard in the cablegram of Moshe Shertok, its Foreign Secretary, dated 15 May 1948 (UN Doc.S/747). Chapter 4 of Part I C of the resolution also stated:

> The provisions of chapters 1 (Holy Places, religious buildings and sites) and 2 (religious and minority rights) shall be under the guarantee of the United Nations, and no modification shall be made in them without the assent of the General Assembly of the United Nations. Any Member of the United Nations shall have the right to bring to the attention of the General Assembly any infraction or danger of infraction of any of these stipulations, and the General Assembly may thereupon make such recommendations as it may deem proper in the circumstances. Any dispute relating to the application or the interpretation of this declaration shall be referred, at the request of either party, to the International Court of Justice, unless the parties agree to another mode of settlement.

What are the conservatory measures that should be taken? The answer is found in UN resolutions. These concern (a) the enforcement of the international legal status of Jerusalem laid down in resolutions 181 (II), 194 (III) and 303 (IV) which would require the evacuation by Israel of the *corpus separatum*, (b) the repatriation of the Palestinian refugees which is called for in a long line of resolutions since 1948, (c) the rescission of all measures which have altered the administration, the demography and land ownership of Jerusalem, and finally (d) the dismantling of settlements as called for by Security Council resolution 465 of 1 March 1980. The annulment of Israeli colonization would necessitate the withdrawal of the settlers that Israel brought to colonize Jerusalem in the same way as all Israeli settlers are required to be withdrawn from Sinai under Article 1 of the Egyptian-Israeli Peace Treaty.

Obviously, the implementation of the conservatory measures suggested above would not only preserve and restore the situation in Jerusalem but would also greatly facilitate the eventual settlement of the problem of the Holy City.

It goes without saying that being a belligerent occupier and possessing no rights whatsoever in Jerusalem, Israel cannot lawfully resist the adoption and implementation of conservatory measures intended to rescind its unlawful actions in the Holy City.

Temporary International Authority

The implementation of the conservatory measures mentioned above would require the creation of a Temporary International Authority to supervise the operation. Such an Authority would, in addition, be charged with the function of administering the City of Jerusalem.

Tripartite Communal Council

Following the implementation of the conservatory measures, a Tripartite Communal Council would succeed to the Temporary International Authority for the purpose of administering the City of Jerusalem pending a final settlement of the problem of Jerusalem and the Palestine question.

These two bodies, namely the Temporary International Authority and the Tripartite Communal Council, would be set up under the authority of the Security Council or the General Assembly which would define their composition, competence and functions.

The concept underlying the proposed Tripartite Communal Council is based on the consideration that Jerusalem is sacred to the three monotheistic religions. Although the number of Jews in the world (fourteen million) as compared with Christians (more than one billion) and Moslems (about seven hundred million) represents less than one per cent of the number of Christians and Moslems, yet it may constitute a gesture of goodwill and brotherhood, in view of the religious and historic significance of Jerusalem to the three faiths, to recognize a right of equal participation in its administration to each of the three main communities.

It is relevant to mention in this connection that there exists a precedent for a tripartite communal representation in the Advisory Council for Palestine which was set up in 1920 by the British Mandatory Government and which functioned until the promulgation of the Palestine Order-in-Council of 1922. In addition to official members, the Advisory Council comprised ten members named by the British High Commissioner, four of whom were Moslem Arabs, three Christian Arabs and three Jews.

The principle of equal communal representation was adopted by the Trusteeship Council in 1950 for the composition of the Legislative Council which was envisaged under resolution 181 (II) for the City of Jerusalem. Originally it was provided by the resolution that the Legislative Council would be elected by adult residents of the city on the basis of universal suffrage and proportional representation. However, the Statute which was approved on 4 April 1950 by the Trusteeship Council substituted the system of equal communal representation for that of universal suffrage and proportional representation. Article 21 of the Statute provided that the Legislative Council shall consist of twenty-five elected members and not more than fifteen designated members. Three electoral colleges, one Christian, one Moslem and one Jewish, shall each elect eight members and a fourth college composed of those who do not register with any of the three other colleges shall elect one member. As to the non-elected members, they would be designated by the heads of the principal religious communities representing the Christian, Moslem and Jewish religions.

It is necessary to emphasize that the proposal for a Tripartite Communal Council does not aim at prejudicing the future political structure for the administration of Jerusalem under a final settlement of the Palestine question. Whatever might be the eventual solution of the Palestine question, the communal administrative structure suggested above could then be modified, adjusted or abrogated in the light of the final settlement.

It will be objected that while the conservatory measures herein suggested might receive full support from the UN, the basic obstacles to their implementation would remain: Israel would oppose them and the US Government would not co-operate in their implementation.

As regards Israel, there is no doubt that one can expect a stiff and determined opposition on its part. It is axiomatic that the implementation of any measures that aim at the rescission of its actions in Jerusalem requires the exercise of coercion. This is recognized by all observers. Dr John Davis, former Commissioner-General of UNRWA (United Nations Relief and Works Agency for Palestine Refugees), observed: 'in the end one must even be prepared to use corrective measures on Israel against her will'.[4] Israel has opposed and thwarted the implementation of each and every resolution adopted by the UN on Jerusalem. It has destroyed the prestige and credibility of the international organization. If the world community wants to restore justice and legality in Jerusalem, it must be prepared to have recourse to *all* the means envisaged by the Charter of the UN, including the use of force, for the implementation of UN decisions.

US Policy

Turning to the obstacle arising from US policy and the eventuality of US non-co-operation in, or even opposition to, the measures of coercion that will unavoidably be needed against Israel, the position may not be now, as in the past, one of full and unqualified support of Israeli actions. Although one cannot yet speak of a complete reversal of attitude, there have been of late certain signs indicative of change in US Middle Eastern policy.

We can better appreciate the situation if we contrast the conflicting factors which are at play.

There are two main factors on the negative side.

There is first the fact that US policy is mortgaged to Israel's will and pleasure since the US Government accepted important restrictions on its freedom of diplomatic action in regard to the settlement of the Arab-Israeli conflict and the non-recognition of the Palestine Liberation Organization. These restrictions are contained in a package of political and military commitments which the US assumed in favour of Israel in connection with the second Sinai Agreement of September 1975 – this being one of the regrettable achievements of Secretary of State, Dr Henry Kissinger. These commitments, however, do not contain any specific constrictions on US freedom of diplomatic action with respect to Jerusalem.

There is also on the negative side the powerful Zionist Jewish/Israeli lobby which largely influences US policy concerning the Arab-Israeli conflict. The 1980 presidential elections have shown that this conflict cannot be insulated from internal American politics for the reason that the Zionist Jewish/Israeli lobby seeks to extract from all candidates positive assurances and even future commitments of support for Israel. Even the question of Jerusalem, as we have seen, was shamelessly exploited in these elections.

On the other hand, there exist factors on the positive side which are of recent vintage.

As a result of the developments in Iran (seizure of American hostages) and in Afghanistan (Soviet intervention), the US has resorted to international legal machinery to the use of which it had shown a marked indifference, even opposition, in the past in regard to the Palestine question. It has appealed to the International Court of Justice for a decision on the question of the hostages detained by Iran, whereas, it will be recalled, it opposed and defeated in 1947 several requests made to the General Assembly to seek from the Court an advisory opinion on important juridical issues involved in the Palestine question. Moreover, it has resorted to the Security Council and the General Assembly to seek support from world opinion in regard to events in those two countries, thereby showing the importance it now attaches to the legal, moral and political value of UN resolutions. There are scores of UN resolutions adopted by the Security Council and the General Assembly on the Palestine question, on Jerusalem, on the Palestinian refugees, on the rescission of Israeli actions that are crying for execution and which have not been implemented precisely by reason of Israel's opposition and US acquiescence in Israel's non-compliance. The conservatory measures herein suggested all rest on a strong legal and moral basis and on UN resolutions and it might perhaps be difficult for the US Government to oppose their implementation.

Moreover, other developments which have occurred in recent years, such as the Arab oil embargo in 1973, the generally hostile reaction to the Camp David accords which were sponsored by President Carter for the benefit of Israel, the coolness of the Arab States to US efforts to mobilize them in the face of potential dangers to its vital interests in the Persian Gulf area – all of which may be attributed to US partiality in favour of Israel – have highlighted the grave perils to America's interests resulting from the US administration's misguided support of Israel. The apparent acquiescence in the Israeli domination of Jerusalem which was displayed by the American President's insistence on deleting all references to Jerusalem in the Security Council resolution of 1 March 1980 that condemned Israeli settlements could, if it were to become a principle of US policy, create a most explosive issue between the US and the Arab and Islamic world. The feelings of the Arab and Islamic world concerning US policy were expressed in an editorial in a British magazine which asked: 'Is Jerusalem of less concern to the world than Kabul? Are a million Palestinians under Israeli domination less deserving of sympathy than 50 Americans in Tehran?'[5]

There seems to exist a greater awareness at present of the basic issues and values involved in the Arab-Israeli conflict as is evident from certain criticisms directed at US policy. Two citations in this regard may be of relevance.

The first comes from Mr Nahum Goldmann, Founder President of the World Jewish Congress and former President of the World Zionist Organization. After blaming Israel for its 'intransigence' and pointing out that 'Israel's rigid policy has not changed radically from Ben Gurion to Begin', he goes on to criticize the US in these terms:

> I have maintained for years that America, by its reluctance to influence Israel and through having given in to too many Israeli demands — for instance, with regard to the Jarring mission, the Rogers Plan, etc. — not only failed to help Israel but harmed it in the long run.[6]

The second citation comes from Mr George W. Ball, formerly US Under-Secretary of State. Commenting upon the danger which Russia's armed intervention in Afghanistan represents to US oil interests in the Gulf, he says:

> We cannot defend the eastern shore of the Gulf without the full cooperation of the Arab states on the western shore.
> That means we can no longer doltishly ignore the prime political reality of the Palestinian issue. So far we have persistently approached the Middle Eastern problem from the wrong side, spending enormous political capital to settle the Israeli-Egyptian quarrel, which has little to do with oil, while in the process inflaming the Israeli-Palestinian dispute, which critically affects U.S. relations with the oil-producing countries. But we cannot realistically expect those Arab nations to risk close identification with us by giving the United States bases on their soil or cooperating in military planning while we continue to subsidize Israeli colonialism on the West Bank and the Gaza Strip and condone by inaction the Begin government's cynical effort to absorb those areas. Let there be no mistake about it: So long as the United States delays a frontal attack on the Palestinian issue, it is alienating the whole Moslem world, as shattered U.S. Embassies have demonstrated.[7]

Incidentally, it may be remarked that the US annual subsidy to Israeli colonialism was stated by Mr George W. Ball to amount to the equivalent of $7,500 a year for every Jewish family.[8]

The American vote on 1 March 1980 in favour of the Security Council resolution on the dismantling of Israeli settlements, though sabotaged by the White House two days later under the influence of Israel and the Zionist/Jewish lobby, appears to be the result of the increasing awareness of the immense damage done to the higher interests of the American nation in the Arab world by US pro-Israeli policy. One should not, therefore, despair of seeing the US bringing its support to measures of coercion intended to secure Israel's respect of international law and obedience to UN resolutions.

The US carries a great responsibility in the case of Jerusalem and one ventures to hope that it will discharge it in a manner compatible with its traditions of fairness and justice.

Notes

1. Has any respect been shown in the Palestinian question to 'the principles of justice and international law' or to 'human rights and fundamental freedoms' which are mentioned in Article 1 of the Charter?

2. There exist over 260 UN resolutions on the Palestine question and Jerusalem, all of which, without exception, were flouted by Israel.

3. In 1947 the General Assembly denied several requests for an advisory opinion of the International Court of Justice on the Palestine question: see UN Docs.A/AC 14/21, 14 October 1947; A/AC 14/24, 16 October 1947; A/AC 14/25, 16 October 1947; and A/AC 14/32, 11 November 1947.

4. John H. Davis, *The Evasive Peace* (John Murray, London, 1968), p. 107.

5. *Middle East International*, London, 18 January 1980, p. 1.

6. Nahum Goldmann, 'Zionist Ideology and the Reality of Israel', *Foreign Affairs* (Fall 1978), p. 81.

7. *International Herald Tribune*, 25 January 1980.

8. George W. Ball, 'The Coming Crisis in Israeli-American Relations', *Foreign Affairs* (Winter 1979/80), p. 246.

APPENDICES

I
CHRONOLOGY OF JERUSALEM

		Years of occupation
Canaanites	From around 1800 BC or earlier until the capture of the city by David in about 1000 BC	800
Israelites (with intermittent occupations of the city by the Egyptians, the Philistines, the Syrians and the Assyrians)	From 1000 BC to capture of the city by the Babylonians in 587 BC	413
Babylonians	From 587 to 538 BC	50
Persians	From capture of the city by Cyrus to Greek conquest: 538 to 332 BC	206
Greeks	Alexander's conquest of the city to its emancipation by the Maccabees: 332 to 141 BC	191
Jews	Maccabean rule: 141 to 63 BC	78
Pagan Romans	Roman conquest of the city to fall of paganism: 63 BC to AD 323	386
Christians	From Constantine to Persian conquest: 323 to 614	291
Persians	Persian rule: 614 to 628	14
Christians	Reconquest of the city by Byzantines: 628 to 638	10
Arabs	Conquest by the Arabs: 638 to 1072	434

Turks	Seizure of the city by the Turks: 1072 to 1092	20
Arabs	Reconquest of the city by Arabs: 1092 to 1099	7
Christians	Latin Kingdom of Jerusalem: 1099 to 1187	88
Arabs	Reconquest of the city by the Arabs: 1187 to 1229	42
Christians	City ceded by treaty for ten years to Frederick II: 1229 to 1239	10
Arabs	Revived Arab rule: 1239 to 1517	278
Turks	Occupation by the Ottoman Turks: 1517 to 1831	314
Arabs	Occupation of Jerusalem by Mohamed Ali and Egyptian rule from 1831 to 1841	10
Turks	Restoration of Turkish rule: 1841 to 1917	76
Christians	British occupation and mandate: 1917 to 1948	31
Israelis and Arabs	New City of Jerusalem occupied by Israel and Old City occupied by Jordan: 1948 to 1967	19
Israelis	Capture of Old City by Israel in 1967	

II
CHRISTIAN HOLY PLACES AND RELIGIOUS SHRINES IN JERUSALEM AND ITS VICINITY

1. Church of the Holy Sepulchre
2. The Via Dolorosa which includes the nine Stations of the Cross
3. The Cenacle
4. The Garden of Gethsemane
5. The Tomb of the Blessed Virgin
6. The Mount of Olives
7. The Garden Tomb (considered by many Protestants to be the Tomb of Christ)
8. Bethany
9. Bethlehem (Church of the Nativity, Milk Grotto and Shepherds Field)
10. Ein Karem (birthplace of John the Baptist)
11. Thirty-eight churches of different denominations

III
MOSLEM HOLY PLACES AND RELIGIOUS SHRINES IN JERUSALEM AND ITS VICINITY

1. *Haram Al-Sharif*
2. Mosque of the Dome of the Rock
3. Mosque of Al-Aqsa
4. Al Buraq
5. Thirty-four mosques in various parts of the city
6. David's Tomb

IV
JEWISH HOLY PLACES AND RELIGIOUS SHRINES IN JERUSALEM AND ITS VICINITY

1. The Wailing Wall
2. Various synagogues in the Jewish Quarter of the Old City

V
MUNICIPAL MAP OF JERUSALEM SHOWING ARAB AND JEWISH QUARTERS IN 1948

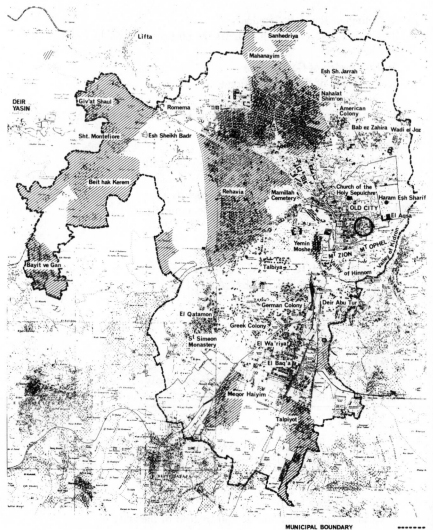

MUNICIPAL BOUNDARY

ARAB QUARTERS

JEWISH QUARTERS

JEWISH QUARTER IN OLD CITY

VI
SCHEDULE OF ARAB AND JEWISH LAND OWNERSHIP IN JERUSALEM IN 1948

Area: New City   19,331 *dunoms**

           Old City   800 *dunoms*

Total Area   20,131 *dunoms*

i) *Land ownership in New City*

Arab-owned	40.00%
Jewish-owned	26.12%
Others (Christian Communities)	13.86%
Government & Municipal	2.90%
Roads and Railways	17.12%

ii) *Land ownership in Old City*

Jewish land ownership in Old City is less than five *dunoms*. The remainder belongs to Christians and Moslems.

---

* One *dunom* equals 1,000 square metres

  4.05 *dunoms* equal one acre

  1,000 *dunoms* equal one square kilometre

  2,590 *dunoms* equal one square mile

Source: Sami Hadawi, *Palestine, Loss of a Heritage* (Naylor Company, San Antonio, Texas, 1963), p. 141. The author was a former Palestine Government Official of the Department of Land Settlement.

VII
EXCERPTS FROM GENERAL ASSEMBLY RESOLUTION 181 (II) of 29 NOVEMBER 1947 CONCERNING THE FUTURE GOVERNMENT OF PALESTINE AND THE INTERNATIONALIZATION OF JERUSALEM

A

The General Assembly,

Having met in special session at the request of the mandatory Power to constitute and instruct a special committee to prepare for the consideration of the question of the future government of Palestine at the second regular session;

Having constituted a Special Committee and instructed it to investigate all questions and issues relevant to the problem of Palestine, and to prepare proposals for the solution of the problem, and

Having received and examined the report of the Special Committee . . .

Recommends to the United Kingdom, as the mandatory Power for Palestine, and to all other Members of the United Nations the adoption and implementation, with regard to the future government of Palestine, of the Plan of Partition with Economic Union set out below . . .

PLAN OF PARTITION WITH ECONOMIC UNION

PART I

Future constitution and government of Palestine

A. TERMINATION OF MANDATE, PARTITION AND INDEPENDENCE

1. The Mandate for Palestine shall terminate as soon as possible but in any case not later than 1 August 1948.

2. The armed forces of the mandatory Power shall be progressively

withdrawn from Palestine, the withdrawal to be completed as soon as possible but in any case not later than 1 August 1948.

The mandatory Power shall advise the Commission, as far in advance as possible, of its intention to terminate the Mandate and to evacuate each area.

The mandatory Power shall use its best endeavours to ensure that an area situated in the territory of the Jewish State, including a seaport and hinterland adequate to provide facilities for a substantial immigration, shall be evacuated at the earliest possible date and in any event not later than 1 February 1948.

3. Independent Arab and Jewish States and the Special International Regime for the City of Jerusalem, set forth in part III of this plan, shall come into existence in Palestine two months after the evacuation of the armed forces of the mandatory Power has been completed but in any case not later than 1 October 1948. The boundaries of the Arab State, the Jewish State, and the City of Jerusalem shall be as described in parts II and III below.

4. The period between the adoption by the General Assembly of its recommendation on the question of Palestine and the establishment of the independence of the Arab and Jewish States shall be a transitional period.

C. DECLARATION

A declaration shall be made to the United Nations by the provisional government of each proposed State before independence. It shall contain *inter alia* the following clauses:

GENERAL PROVISION

The stipulations contained in the declaration are recognized as fundamental laws of the State and no law, regulation or official action shall conflict or interfere with these stipulations, nor shall any law, regulation or official action prevail over them.

Chapter I

Holy Places, religious buildings and sites

1. Existing rights in respect of Holy Places and religious buildings or sites shall not be denied or impaired.

2. In so far as Holy Places are concerned, the liberty of access, visit and transit shall be guaranteed, in conformity with existing rights, to all residents and citizens of the other State and of the City of Jerusalem,

as well as to aliens, without distinction as to nationality, subject to requirements of national security, public order and decorum.

Similarly, freedom of worship shall be guaranteed in conformity with existing rights, subject to the maintenance of public order and decorum.

3. Holy Places and religious buildings or sites shall be preserved. No act shall be permitted which may in any way impair their sacred character. If at any time it appears to the Government that any particular Holy Place, religious building or site is in need of urgent repair, the Government may call upon the community or communities concerned to carry out such repair. The Government may carry it out itself at the expense of the community or communities concerned if no action is taken within a reasonable time.

4. No taxation shall be levied in respect of any Holy Place, religious building or site which was exempt from taxation on the date of the creation of the State.

No change in the incidence of such taxation shall be made which would either discriminate between the owners or occupiers of Holy Places, religious buildings or sites, or would place such owners or occupiers in a position less favourable in relation to the general incidence of taxation than existed at the time of the adoption of the Assembly's recommendations.

5. The Governor of the City of Jerusalem shall have the right to determine whether the provisions of the Constitution of the State in relation to Holy Places, religious buildings and sites within the borders of the State and the religious rights appertaining thereto, are being properly applied and respected, and to make decisions on the basis of existing rights in cases of disputes which may arise between the different religious communities or the rites of a religious community with respect to such places, buildings and sites. He shall receive full co-operation and such privileges and immunities as are necessary for the exercise of his functions in the State.

Chapter 2

Religious and minority rights

1. Freedom of conscience and the free exercise of all forms of worship, subject only to the maintenance of public order and morals, shall be ensured to all.

2. No discrimination of any kind shall be made between the inhabitants on the ground of race, religion, language or sex.

3. All persons within the jurisdiction of the State shall be entitled to

equal protection of the laws.

4. The family law and personal status of the various minorities and their religious interests, including endowments, shall be respected.

5. Except as may be required for the maintenance of public order and good government, no measure shall be taken to obstruct or interfere with the enterprise of religious or charitable bodies of all faiths or to discriminate against any representative or member of these bodies on the ground of his religion or nationality.

6. The State shall ensure adequate primary and secondary education for the Arab and Jewish minority, respectively, in its own language and its cultural traditions.

The right of each community to maintain its own schools for the education of its own members in its own language, while conforming to such educational requirements of a general nature as the State may impose, shall not be denied or impaired. Foreign educational establishments shall continue their activity on the basis of their existing rights.

7. No restriction shall be imposed on the free use by any citizen of the State of any language in private intercourse, in commerce, in religion, in the Press or in publications of any kind, or at public meetings.[1]

8. No expropriation of land owned by an Arab in the Jewish State (by a Jew in the Arab State)[2] shall be allowed except for public purposes. In all cases of expropriation full compensation as fixed by the Supreme Court shall be paid previous to dispossession.

Footnotes
1. The following stipulation shall be added to the declaration concerning the Jewish State: 'In the Jewish State adequate facilities shall be given to the Arab-speaking citizens for the use of their language, either orally or in writing, in the legislature, before the Courts and in the administration.'
2. In the declaration concerning the Arab State, the words 'by an Arab in the Jewish State' should be replaced by the words 'by a Jew in the Arab State'.

Chapter 4

Miscellaneous provisions

1. The provisions of chapters 1 and 2 of the declaration shall be under the guarantee of the United Nations, and no modifications shall be made in them without the assent of the General Assembly of the United Nations. Any Member of the United Nations shall have the right to bring to the attention of the General Assembly any infraction or danger of infraction of any of these stipulations, and the General Assembly may thereupon make such recommendations as it may deem proper in the circumstances.

2. Any dispute relating to the application or the interpretation of this declaration shall be referred, at the request of either party, to the International Court of Justice, unless the parties agree to another mode of settlement.

PART II

Boundaries

[omitted]

PART III

City of Jerusalem

A. SPECIAL REGIME

The City of Jerusalem shall be established as a *corpus separatum* under a special international régime and shall be administered by the United Nations. The Trusteeship Council shall be designated to discharge the responsibilities of the Administering Authority on behalf of the United Nations.

B. BOUNDARIES OF THE CITY

The City of Jerusalem shall include the present municipality of Jerusalem plus the surrounding villages and towns, the most eastern of which shall be Abu Dis; the most southern, Bethlehem; the most western, Ein Karim (including also the built-up area of Motsa); and the most northern Shu'fat, as indicated on the attached sketch-map (annex B).

C. STATUTE OF THE CITY

The Trusteeship Council shall, within five months of the approval of the present plan, elaborate and approve a detailed Statute of the City which shall contain *inter alia* the substance of the following provisions:

1. *Government machinery; special objectives.* The Administering Authority in discharging its administrative obligations shall pursue the following special objectives:

(*a*) To protect and to preserve the unique spiritual and religious interests located in the city of the three great monotheistic faiths throughout the world, Christian, Jewish and Moslem; to this end to ensure that order and peace, and especially religious peace, reign in Jerusalem;

(*b*) To foster co-operation among all the inhabitants of the city in their own interests as well as in order to encourage and support the peaceful development of the mutual relations between the two Palestinian peoples throughout the Holy Land; to promote the security, well-being and any constructive measures of development of the residents, having regard to the special circumstances and customs of the various peoples and communities.

2. *Governor and administrative staff.* A Governor of the City of Jerusalem shall be appointed by the Trusteeship Council and shall be responsible to it. He shall be selected on the basis of special qualifications and without regard to nationality. He shall not, however, be a citizen of either State in Palestine.

The Governor shall represent the United Nations in the City and shall exercise on their behalf all powers of administration, including the conduct of external affairs. He shall be assisted by an administrative staff classed as international officers in the meaning of Article 100 of the Charter and chosen whenever practicable from the residents of the city and of the rest of Palestine on a non-discriminatory basis. A detailed plan for the organization of the administration of the city shall be submitted by the Governor to the Trusteeship Council and duly approved by it.

3. *Local autonomy.* (*a*) The existing local autonomous units in the territory of the city (villages, townships and municipalities) shall enjoy wide powers of local government and administration.

(*b*) The Governor shall study and submit for the consideration and decision of the Trusteeship Council a plan for the establishment of special town units consisting, respectively of the Jewish and Arab sections of new Jerusalem. The new town units shall continue to form part of the present municipality of Jerusalem.

4. *Security measures.* (*a*) The City of Jerusalem shall be demilitarized; its neutrality shall be declared and preserved, and no paramilitary formations, exercises or activities shall be permitted within its borders.

(*b*) Should the administration of the City of Jerusalem be seriously obstructed or prevented by the non-co-operation or interference of one or more sections of the population, the Governor shall have authority to take such measures as may be necessary to restore the effective functioning of the administration.

(*c*) To assist in the maintenance of internal law and order and especially for the protection of the Holy Places and religious buildings and sites in the city, the Governor shall organize a special police force of adequate strength, the members of which shall be recruited outside of Palestine. The Governor shall be empowered to direct such budgetary provision as may be necessary for the maintenance of this force.

5. *Legislative organization.* A Legislative Council, elected by adult residents of the city irrespective of nationality on the basis of universal and secret suffrage and proportional representation, shall have powers of legislation and taxation. No legislative measures shall, however, conflict or interfere with the provisions which will be set forth in the Statute of the City, nor shall any law, regulation, or official action prevail over them. The Statute shall grant to the Governor a right of vetoing bills inconsistent with the provisions referred to in the preceding sentence. It shall also empower him to promulgate temporary ordinances in case the Council fails to adopt in time a bill deemed essential to the normal functioning of the administration.

6. *Administration of justice.* The Statute shall provide for the establishment of an independent judiciary system, including a court of appeal. All the inhabitants of the City shall be subject to it.

7. *Economic union and economic regime.* The City of Jerusalem shall be included in the Economic Union of Palestine and be bound by all stipulations of the undertaking and of any treaties issued therefrom, as well as by the decisions of the Joint Economic Board. The headquarters of the Economic Board shall be established in the territory of the City.

The Statute shall provide for the regulation of economic matters not falling within the regime of the Economic Union, on the basis of equal treatment and non-discrimination for all Members of the United Nations and their nationals.

8. *Freedom of transit and visit; control of residents.* Subject to considerations of security, and of economic welfare as determined by the

Governor under the directions of the Trusteeship Council, freedom of entry into, and residence within, the borders of the City shall be guaranteed for the residents or citizens of the Arab and Jewish States. Immigration into, and residence within, the borders of the city for nationals of other States shall be controlled by the Governor under the directions of the Trusteeship Council.

9. *Relations with the Arab and Jewish States.* Representatives of the Arab and Jewish States shall be accredited to the Governor of the City and charged with the protection of the interests of their States and nationals in connexion with the international administration of the City.

10. *Official languages.* Arabic and Hebrew shall be the official languages of the city. This will not preclude the adoption of one or more additional working languages, as may be required.

11. *Citizenship.* All the residents shall become *ipso facto* citizens of the City of Jerusalem unless they opt for citizenship of the State of which they have been citizens or, if Arabs or Jews, have filed notice of intention to become citizens of the Arab or Jewish State respectively, according to part I, section B, paragraph 9, of this plan.

The Trusteeship Council shall make arrangements for consular protection of the citizens of the City outside its territory.

12. *Freedoms of citizens.* (*a*) Subject only to the requirements of public order and morals, the inhabitants of the City shall be ensured the enjoyment of human rights and fundamental freedoms, including freedom of conscience, religion and worship, language, education, speech and Press, assembly and association, and petition.

(*b*) No discrimination of any kind shall be made between the inhabitants on the grounds of race, religion, language or sex.

(*c*) All persons within the City shall be entitled to equal protection of the laws.

(*d*) The family law and personal status of the various persons and communities and their religious interests, including endowments, shall be respected.

(*e*) Except as may be required for the maintenance of public order and good government, no measure shall be taken to obstruct or interfere with the enterprise of religious or charitable bodies of all faiths or to discriminate against any representative or member of these bodies on the ground of his religion or nationality.

(*f*) The City shall ensure adequate primary and secondary education for the Arab and Jewish communities respectively, in their own languages and in accordance with their cultural traditions.

The right of each community to maintain its own schools for the education of its own members in its own language, while conforming to such educational requirements of a general nature as the City may impose, shall not be denied or impaired. Foreign educational establishments shall continue their activity on the basis of their existing rights.

(g) No restriction shall be imposed on the free use by any inhabitant of the City of any language in private intercourse, in commerce, in the Press or in publications of any kind, or at public meetings.

13. *Holy Places.* (a) Existing rights in respect of Holy Places and religious buildings or sites shall not be denied or impaired.

(b) Free access to the Holy Places and religious buildings or sites and the free exercise of worship shall be secured in conformity with existing rights and subject to the requirements of public order and decorum.

(c) Holy Places and religious buildings or sites shall be preserved. No act shall be permitted which may in any way impair their sacred character. If at any time it appears to the Governor that any particular Holy Place, religious building or site is in need of urgent repair, the Governor may call upon the community or communities concerned to carry out such repair. The Governor may carry it out himself at the expense of the community or communities concerned if no action is taken within a reasonable time.

(d) No taxation shall be levied in respect of any Holy Place, religious building or site which was exempt from taxation on the date of the creation of the City. No change in the incidence of such taxation shall be made which would either discriminate between the owners or occupiers of Holy Places, religious buildings or sites, or would place such owners or occupiers in a position less favourable in relation to the general incidence of taxation than existed at the time of the adoption of the Assembly's recommendations.

14. *Special powers of the Governor in respect of the Holy Places, religious buildings and sites in the City and in any part of Palestine.* (a) The protection of the Holy Places, religious buildings and sites located in the City of Jerusalem shall be a special concern of the Governor.

(b) With relation to such places, buildings and sites in Palestine outside the city, the Governor shall determine, on the ground of powers granted to him by the Constitutions of both States, whether the provisions of the Constitutions of the Arab and Jewish States in Palestine dealing therewith and the religious rights appertaining thereto are being properly applied and respected.

(c) The Governor shall also be empowered to make decisions on the basis of existing rights in cases of disputes which may arise between the different religious communities or the rites of a religious community in respect of the Holy Places, religious buildings and sites in any part of Palestine.

In this task he may be assisted by a consultative council of representatives of different denominations acting in an advisory capacity.

D. DURATION OF THE SPECIAL REGIME

The Statute elaborated by the Trusteeship Council on the aforementioned principles shall come into force not later than 1 October 1948. It shall remain in force in the first instance for a period of ten years, unless the Trusteeship Council finds it necessary to undertake a re-examination of these provisions at an earlier date. After the expiration of this period the whole scheme shall be subject to re-examination by the Trusteeship Council in the light of the experience acquired with its functioning. The residents of the City shall be then free to express by means of a referendum their wishes as to possible modifications of the régime of the City.

PART IV

Capitulations

States whose nationals have in the past enjoyed in Palestine the privileges and immunities of foreigners, including the benefits of consular jurisdiction and protection, as formerly enjoyed by capitulation or usage in the Ottoman Empire, are invited to renounce any right pertaining to them to the re-establishment of such privileges and immunities in the proposed Arab and Jewish States and the City of Jerusalem.

VIII
MAP OF *CORPUS SEPARATUM* OF JERUSALEM IN ACCORDANCE WITH GENERAL ASSEMBLY RESOLUTION 181 (11) OF 29 NOVEMBER 1947

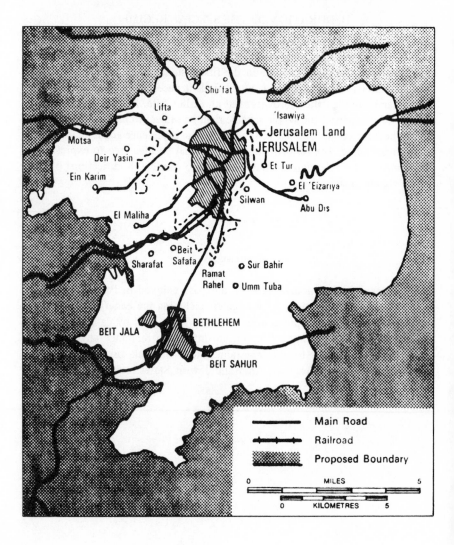

IX

RESOLUTION 194 (III) OF THE GENERAL ASSEMBLY DATED 11 DECEMBER 1948 CONCERNING THE CONCILIATION COMMISSION, THE INTERNATIONAL REGIME OF JERUSALEM, AND THE RETURN OF REFUGEES

The General Assembly,

Having considered further the situation in Palestine,

1. *Expresses* its deep appreciation of the progress achieved through the good offices of the late United Nations Mediator in promoting a peaceful adjustment of the future situation of Palestine, for which cause he sacrificed his life; and

Extends its thanks to the Acting Mediator and his staff for their continued efforts and devotion to duty in Palestine;

2. *Establishes* a Conciliation Commission consisting of three States Members of the United Nations which shall have the following functions:

(*a*) To assume, in so far as it considers necessary in existing circumstances, the functions given to the United Nations Mediator on Palestine by resolution 186 (S-2) of the General Assembly of 14 May 1948;

(*b*) To carry out the specific functions and directives given to it by the present resolution and such additional functions and directives as may be given to it by the General Assembly or by the Security Council;

(*c*) To undertake, upon the request of the Security Council, any of the functions now assigned to the United Nations Mediator on Palestine or to the United Nations Truce Commission by resolutions of the Security Council; upon such request to the Conciliation Commission by the Security Council with respect to all the remaining functions of the United Nations Mediator on Palestine under Security Council resolutions, the office of the Mediator shall be terminated;

3. *Decides* that a Committee of the Assembly, consisting of China,

France, the Union of Soviet Socialist Republics, the United Kingdom and the United States of America, shall present, before the end of the first part of the present session of the General Assembly, for the approval of the Assembly, a proposal concerning the names of the three States which will constitute the Conciliation Commission;

4. *Requests* the Commission to begin its functions at once, with a view to the establishment of contact between the parties themselves and the Commission at the earliest possible date;

5. *Calls upon* the Governments and authorities concerned to extend the scope of the negotiations provided for in the Security Council's resolution of 16 November 1948 and to seek agreement by negotiations conducted either with the Conciliation Commission or directly, with a view to the final settlement of all questions outstanding between them;

6. *Instructs* the Conciliation Commission to take steps to assist the Governments and authorities concerned to achieve a final settlement of all questions outstanding between them;

7. *Resolves* that the Holy Places — including Nazareth — religious buildings and sites in Palestine should be protected and free access to them assured, in accordance with existing rights and historical practice; that arrangements to this end should be under effective United Nations supervision; that the United Nations Conciliation Commission, in presenting to the fourth regular session of the General Assembly its detailed proposals for a permanent international regime for the territory of Jerusalem, should include recommendations concerning the Holy Places in that territory; that with regard to the Holy Places in the rest of Palestine the Commission should call upon the political authorities of the areas concerned to give appropriate formal guarantees as to the protection of the Holy Places and access to them; and that these undertakings should be presented to the General Assembly for approval;

8. *Resolves* that, in view of its association with three world religions, the Jerusalem area, including the present municipality of Jerusalem *plus* the surrounding villages and towns, the most eastern of which shall be Abu Dis; the most southern, Bethlehem; the most western, Ein Karim (including also the built-up area of Motsa); and the most northern Shu'fat, should be accorded special and separate treatment from the rest of Palestine and should be placed under effective United Nations control;

Requests the Security Council to take further steps to ensure the demilitarization of Jerusalem at the earliest possible date;

Instructs the Commission to present to the fourth regular session of the General Assembly detailed proposals for a permanent international regime for the Jerusalem area which shall provide for the maximum local autonomy for distinctive groups consistent with the special international status of the Jerusalem area;

The Conciliation Commission is authorized to appoint a United Nations representative, who shall co-operate with the local authorities with respect to the interim administration of the Jerusalem area;

9. *Resolves* that, pending agreement on more detailed arrangements among the Governments and authorities concerned, the freest possible access to Jerusalem by road, rail or air should be accorded to all inhabitants of Palestine;

Instructs the Conciliation Commission to report immediately to the Security Council, for appropriate action by that organ, any attempt by any party to impede such access;

10. *Instructs* the Conciliation Commission to seek arrangements among the Governments and authorities concerned which will facilitate the economic development of the area, including arrangements for access to ports and airfields and the use of transportation and communication facilities;

11. *Resolves* that the refugees wishing to return to their homes and live at peace with their neighbours should be permitted to do so at the earliest practicable date, and that compensation should be paid for the property of those choosing not to return and for loss of or damage to property which, under principles of international law or in equity, should be made good by the Governments or authorities responsible;

Instructs the Conciliation Commission to facilitate the repatriation, resettlement and economic and social rehabilitation of the refugees and the payment of compensation, and to maintain close relations with the Director of the United Nations Relief for Palestine Refugees and, through him, with the appropriate organs and agencies of the United Nations;

12. *Authorizes* the Conciliation Commission to appoint such subsidiary bodies and to employ such technical experts, acting under its authority, as it may find necessary for the effective discharge of its functions and responsibilities under the present resolution;

The Conciliation Commission will have its official headquarters at Jerusalem. The authorities responsible for maintaining order in Jerusalem will be responsible for taking all measures necessary to ensure the security of the Commission. The Secretary-General will provide a limited number of guards for the protection of the staff and premises of the Commission;

13. *Instructs* the Conciliation Commission to render progress reports periodically to the Secretary-General for transmission to the Security Council and to the Members of the United Nations;

14. *Calls upon* all Governments and authorities concerned to co-operate with the Conciliation Commission and to take all possible steps to assist in the implementation of the present resolution;

15. *Requests* the Secretary-General to provide the necessary staff and facilities and to make appropriate arrangements to provide the necessary funds required in carrying out the terms of the present resolution.

X

RESOLUTION 273 (III) OF THE GENERAL ASSEMBLY DATED 11 MAY 1949 CONCERNING THE ADMISSION OF ISRAEL TO UN MEMBERSHIP

Having received the report of the Security Council on the application of Israel for membership in the United Nations,[6]

Noting that, in the judgement of the Security Council, Israel is a peace-loving State and is able and willing to carry out the obligations contained in the Charter,

Noting that the Security Council has recommended to the General Assembly that it admit Israel to membership in the United Nations,

Noting furthermore the declaration by the State of Israel that it "unreservedly accepts the obligations of the United Nations Charter and undertakes to honour them from the day when it becomes a Member of the United Nations",[7]

Recalling its resolutions of 29 November 1947[8] and 11 December 1948[9] and taking note of the declarations and explanations made by the representative of the Government of Israel[10] before the *ad hoc* Political Committee in respect of the implementation of the said resolutions,

The General Assembly,

Acting in discharge of its functions under Article 4 of the Charter and rule 125 of its rules of procedure,

1. *Decides* that Israel is a peace-loving State which accepts the obligations contained in the Charter and is able and willing to carry out those obligations;

2. *Decides* to admit Israel to membership in the United Nations.

207th plenary meeting,
11 May 1949.

6. See document A/818.

7. See document S/1093.

8. See *Resolutions adopted by the General Assembly* during its second session, pages 131-132.

9. See *Resolutions adopted by the General Assembly* during Part I of its third session, pages 21-25.

10. See documents A/AC.24/SR.45-48, 50 and 51.

RESOLUTION 303 (IV) OF THE GENERAL ASSEMBLY DATED 9 DECEMBER 1949 CONCERNING THE INTERNATIONAL REGIME FOR JERUSALEM

The General Assembly,

Having regard to its resolutions 181 (II) of 29 November 1947 and 194 (III) of 11 December 1948,

Having studied the reports of the United Nations Conciliation Commission for Palestine set up under the latter resolution,

I

Decides, In relation to Jerusalem,

Believing that the principles underlying the previous resolutions concerning this matter, and in particular its resolution of 29 November 1947, represent a just and equitable settlement of the question.

1. To restate, therefore, its intention that Jerusalem should be placed under a permanent international regime, which should envisage appropriate guarantees for the protection of the Holy Places, both within and outside Jerusalem, and to confirm specifically the following provisions of General Assembly Resolution 181 (II). (1) the City of Jerusalem shall be established as a *corpus separatum* under a special international regime and shall be administered by the United Nations; (2) The Trusteeship Council shall be designated to discharge the responsibilities of the Administering Authority . . .; and (3) the City of Jerusalem shall include the present municipality of Jerusalem plus the surrounding villages and towns, the most eastern of which shall be Abu Dis; the most southern, Bethlehem; the most western Ein Karem (including also the built-up area of Motsa); and the most northern, Shu'fat, as indicated on the attached sketch-map;

2. To request for this purpose that the Trusteeship Council at its next session, whether special or regular, complete the preparation of the Statute of Jerusalem, omitting the new inapplicable provisions, such as articles 32 and 39, and, without prejudice to the fundamental

principles of the international regime for Jerusalem set forth in General Assembly resolution 181 (II) introducing therein amendments in the direction of its greater democratization, approve the Statute, and proceed immediately with its implementation. The Trusteeship Council shall not allow any actions taken by any interested Government or Governments to divert it from adopting and implementing the Statute of Jerusalem;

II

Calls upon the States concerned to make formal undertakings, at an early date and in the light of their obligations as Members of the United Nations, that they will approach these matters with good will and be guided by the terms of the present resolution.

XII
RESOLUTION 2253 (ES–V) OF THE GENERAL ASSEMBLY DATED 4 JULY 1967 CONCERNING MEASURES TAKEN BY ISRAEL TO CHANGE THE STATUS OF JERUSALEM

The General Assembly,

Deeply concerned at the situation prevailing in Jerusalem as a result of the measures taken by Israel to change the status of the City,

1. *Considers* that these measures are invalid;

2. *Calls upon* Israel to rescind all measures already taken and to desist forthwith from taking any action which would alter the status of Jerusalem;

3. *Requests* the Secretary-General to report to the General Assembly and the Security Council on the situation and on the implementation of the present resolution not later than one week from its adoption.

1548th plenary meeting,
4 July 1967.

XIII
RESOLUTION 2254 (ES–V) OF THE GENERAL ASSEMBLY DATED 14 JULY 1967 CONCERNING MEASURES TAKEN BY ISRAEL TO CHANGE THE STATUS OF JERUSALEM

The General Assembly,

Recalling its resolution 2253 (ES-V) of 4 July 1967,

Having received the report submitted by the Secretary-General,

Taking note with the deepest regret and concern of the non-compliance by Israel with resolution 2253 (ES-V),

1. *Deplores* the failure of Israel to implement General Assembly resolution 2253 (ES-V);

2. *Reiterates* its call to Israel in that resolution to rescind all measures already taken and to desist forthwith from taking any action which would alter the status of Jerusalem;

3. *Requests* the Secretary-General to report to the Security Council and the General Assembly on the situation and on the implementation of the present resolution.

1554th plenary meeting,
14 July 1967.

XIV

RESOLUTION 242 OF THE SECURITY COUNCIL DATED 22 NOVEMBER 1967 CONCERNING WITHDRAWAL OF ISRAELI ARMED FORCES AND TERMINATION OF BELLIGERENCY

The Security Council,

Expressing its continuing concern with the grave situation in the Middle East,

Emphasizing the inadmissibility of the acquisition of territory by war and the need to work for a just and lasting peace in which every State in the area can live in security,

Emphasizing further that all Member States in their acceptance of the Charter of the United Nations have undertaken a commitment to act in accordance with Article 2 of the Charter,

1. *Affirms* that the fulfilment of Charter principles requires the establishment of a just and lasting peace in the Middle East which should include the application of both the following principles:

i. Withdrawal of Israel armed forces from territories occupied in the recent conflict;

ii. Termination of all claims or states of belligerency and respect for and acknowledgement of the sovereignty, territorial integrity and political independence of every State in the area and their right to live in peace within secure and recognized boundaries free from threats or acts of force;

2. *Affirms further* the necessity

(*a*) For guaranteeing freedom of navigation through international waterways in the area;

(*b*) For achieving a just settlement of the refugee problem;

(*c*) For guaranteeing the territorial inviolability and political independence of every State in the area, through measures including the establishment of demilitarized zones;

3. *Requests* the Secretary-General to designate a Special Representative to proceed to the Middle East to establish and maintain contacts

with the States concerned in order to promote agreement and assist efforts to achieve a peaceful and accepted settlement in accordance with the provisions and principles in this resolution;

4. *Requests* the Secretary-General to report to the Security Council on the progress of the efforts of the Special Representative as soon as possible.

Adopted unanimously at the 1382nd meeting.

XV
RESOLUTION 252 OF THE SECURITY COUNCIL DATED 21 MAY 1968 CONCERNING MEASURES TAKEN BY ISRAEL TO CHANGE THE STATUS OF JERUSALEM

The Security Council,

Recalling General Assembly resolutions 2253 (ES-V) and 2254 (ES-V) of 4 and 14 July 1967,

Having considered the letter (S/8560) of the Permanent Representative of Jordan on the situation in Jerusalem and the report of the Secretary-General (S/8146),

Having heard the statements made before the Council,

Noting that since the adoption of the above-mentioned resolutions, Israel has taken further measures and actions in contravention of those resolutions,

Bearing in mind the need to work for a just and lasting peace,

Reaffirming that acquisition of territory by military conquest is inadmissible,

1. *Deplores* the failure of Israel to comply with the General Assembly resolutions mentioned above;

2. *Considers* that all legislative and administrative measures and actions taken by Israel, including expropriation of land and properties thereon, which tend to change the legal status of Jerusalem are invalid and cannot change that status;

3. *Urgently calls upon* Israel to rescind all such measures already taken and to desist forthwith from taking any further action which tends to change the status of Jerusalem;

4. *Requests* the Secretary-General to report to the Security Council on the implementation of the present resolution.

XVI
RESOLUTION 267 OF THE SECURITY COUNCIL DATED 3 JULY 1969 CONCERNING MEASURES TAKEN BY ISRAEL TO CHANGE THE STATUS OF JERUSALEM

The Security Council,

Recalling its resolution 252 of 21 May 1968 and the earlier General Assembly resolutions 2253 (ES-V) and 2254 (ES-V) of 4 and 14 July 1967 respectively concerning measures and actions by Israel affecting the status of the City of Jerusalem,

Having heard the statements of the parties concerned on the question,

Noting that since the adoption of the above-mentioned resolutions Israel has taken further measures tending to change the status of the City of Jerusalem,

Reaffirming the established principle that acquisition of territory by military conquest is inadmissible,

1. *Reaffirms* its resolution 252 (1968);

2. *Deplores* the failure of Israel to show any regard for the General Assembly and Security Council resolutions mentioned above;

3. *Censures* in the strongest terms all measures taken to change the status of the City of Jerusalem;

4. *Confirms* that all legislative and administrative measures and actions by Israel which purport to alter the status of Jerusalem including expropriation of land and properties thereon are invalid and cannot change that status;

5. *Urgently calls* once more upon Israel to rescind forthwith all measures taken by it which may tend to change the status of the City of Jerusalem, and in future to refrain from all actions likely to have such an effect;

6. *Requests* Israel to inform the Security Council without any further delay of its intentions with regard to the implementation of the provisions of this resolution;

7. *Determines* that, in the event of a negative response or no response

from Israel, the Security Council shall reconvene without delay to consider what further action should be taken in this matter;

8. *Requests* the Secretary-General to report to the Security Council on the implementation of this resolution.

XVII
RESOLUTION 271 OF THE SECURITY COUNCIL DATED 15 SEPTEMBER 1969 CONCERNING ARSON AT AL AQSA MOSQUE AND THE STATUS OF JERUSALEM

The Security Council,

Grieved at the extensive damage caused by arson to the Holy Al Aqsa Mosque in Jerusalem on 21 August 1969 under the military occupation of Israel,

Mindful of the consequent loss to human culture,

Having heard the statements made before the Council reflecting the universal outrage caused by the act of sacrilege in one of the most venerated shrines of mankind,

Recalling its resolutions 252 (1968) of 21 May 1968 and 267 (1969) of 3 July 1969 and the earlier General Assembly resolutions 2253 (ES-V) and 2254 (ES-V) of 4 and 14 July 1967, respectively, concerning measures and actions by Israel affecting the status of the City of Jerusalem,

Reaffirming the established principle that acquisition of territory by military conquest is inadmissible,

1. *Reaffirms* its resolutions 252 (1968) and 267 (1969);

2. *Recognizes* that any act of destruction or profanation of the Holy Places, religious buildings and sites in Jerusalem or any encouragement of, or connivance at, any such act may seriously endanger international peace and security;

3. *Determines* that the execrable act of desecration and profanation of the Holy Al Aqsa Mosque emphasizes the immediate necessity of Israel's desisting from acting in violation of the aforesaid resolutions and rescinding forthwith all measures and actions taken by it designed to alter the status of Jerusalem;

4. *Calls upon* Israel scrupulously to observe the provisions of the Geneva Conventions[16] and international law governing military occu-

16. Geneva Conventions of 12 August 1949 (United Nations, *Treaty Series*, vol. 75 (1950), Nos. 970-973).

pation and to refrain from causing any hindrance to the discharge of the established functions of the Supreme Moslem Council of Jerusalem, including any co-operation that Council may desire from countries with predominantly Moslem population and from Moslem communities in relation to its plans for the maintenance and repair of the Islamic Holy Places in Jerusalem;

5. *Condemns* the failure of Israel to comply with the aforementioned resolutions and calls upon it to implement forthwith the provisions of these resolutions;

6. *Reiterates* the determination in paragraph 7 of resolution 267 (1969) that, in the event of a negative response or no response, the Security Council shall convene without delay to consider what further action should be taken in this matter;

7. *Requests* the Secretary-General to follow closely the implementation of the present resolution and to report thereon to the Security Council at the earliest possible date.

> *Adopted at the 1512th meeting by 11 votes to none,*
> *with 4 abstentions (Colombia, Finland, Paraguay,*
> *United States of America).*

XVIII
RESOLUTION 298 OF THE SECURITY COUNCIL DATED 25 SEPTEMBER 1971 CONCERNING MEASURES TAKEN BY ISRAEL TO CHANGE THE STATUS OF JERUSALEM

The Security Council,

Recalling its resolutions 252 (1968) and 267 (1969) and the earlier General Assembly resolutions 2253 (ES-V) and 2254 (ES-V) of July 1967 concerning measures and actions by Israel designed to change the status of the Israeli-occupied section of Jerusalem,

Having considered the letter of the Permanent Representative of Jordan on the situation in Jerusalem (S/10313) and the reports of the Secretary-General (S/8052, S/8146, S/9149 and Add.1, S/9537 and S/10124 and Add. 1 and 2), and having heard the statements of the parties concerned on the question,

Reaffirming the principle that acquisition of territory by military conquest is inadmissible,

Noting with concern the non-compliance by Israel with the above-mentioned resolutions,

Noting with concern further that since the adoption of the above-mentioned resolutions Israel has taken further measures designed to change the status and character of the occupied section of Jerusalem,

1. *Reaffirms* Security Council resolutions 252 (1968) and 267 (1969);

2. *Deplores* the failure of Israel to respect the previous resolutions adopted by the United Nations concerning measures and actions by Israel purporting to affect the status of the city of Jerusalem;

3. *Confirms* in the clearest possible terms that all legislative and administrative actions taken by Israel to change the status of the city of Jerusalem including expropriation of land and properties, transfer of populations and legislation aimed at the incorporation of the occupied section are totally invalid and cannot change that status;

4. *Urgently calls upon* Israel to rescind all previous measures and actions and to take no further steps in the occupied section of

187

Jerusalem which may purport to change the status of the City, or which would prejudice the rights of the inhabitants and the interests of the international community, or a just and lasting peace;

5. *Requests* the Secretary-General, in consultation with the President of the Security Council and using such instrumentalities as he may choose, including a representative or a mission, to report to the Security Council as appropriate and in any event within 60 days on the implementation of this resolution.

XIX
EXCERPTS FROM RESOLUTION 2851 (XXVI) OF THE GENERAL ASSEMBLY DATED 20 DECEMBER 1971 CONCERNING VIOLATIONS BY ISRAEL OF HUMAN RIGHTS IN THE OCCUPIED TERRITORIES

The General Assembly,

2. *Strongly calls upon* Israel to rescind forthwith all measures and to desist from all policies and practices such as:

(*a*) The annexation of any part of the occupied Arab territories;

(*b*) The establishment of Israeli settlements on those territories and the transfer of parts of its civilian population into the occupied territory;

(*c*) The destruction and demolition of villages, quarters and houses and the confiscation and expropriation of property;

(*d*) The evacuation, transfer, deportation and expulsion of the inhabitants of the occupied Arab territories;

(*e*) The denial of the right of the refugeés and displaced persons to return to their homes;

(*f*) The ill-treatment and torture of prisoners and detainees;

(*g*) Collective punishment;

3. *Calls upon* the Government of Israel to permit all persons who have fled the occupied territories or have been deported or expelled therefrom to return to their homes;

4. *Reaffirms* that all measures taken by Israel to settle the occupied territories, including occupied Jerusalem, are completely null and void;

XX
EXCERPTS FROM RESOLUTION OF THE COMMISSION ON HUMAN RIGHTS OF THE ECONOMIC AND SOCIAL COUNCIL OF THE UN DATED 11 FEBRUARY 1974 CONDEMNING ISRAEL'S POLICY OF ANNEXATION, AND TRANSFER OF POPULATION IN THE OCCUPIED TERRITORIES, INCLUDING JERUSALEM[30]

The Commission on Human Rights,

2. *Deplores* Israel's persistent defiance of the relevant resolutions of the United Nations and its continued policy of violating the basic human rights of the inhabitants of the occupied Arab territories;

3. *Reaffirms* that all measures taken by Israel to change the physical character, the demographic structure and the status of the occupied Arab territories, including occupied Jerusalem, are null and void;

4. *Declares* that Israel's policy of annexation, establishment of settlements and transfer of an alien population to the occupied territories is in contravention of the purposes and principles of the Charter of the United Nations, the principles and provisions of international law concerning occupation, the principles of sovereignty and territorial integrity, and the basic human rights and fundamental freedoms of the people.

30. Adopted at the 1254th meeting, on 11 February 1974, by 21 votes to 1, with 8 abstentions.

XXI
EXCERPTS FROM RESOLUTION OF THE COMMISSION ON HUMAN RIGHTS OF THE ECONOMIC AND SOCIAL COUNCIL OF THE UN DATED 21 FEBRUARY 1975 CONDEMNING ISRAEL'S VIOLATIONS OF HUMAN RIGHTS IN THE OCCUPIED TERRITORIES AND CENSURING ISRAEL'S ACTS IN JERUSALEM

The Commission on Human Rights,

1. *Deplores* Israel's continued grave violations, in the occupied Arab territories, of the basic norms of international law and of the relevant international conventions, in particular the Geneva Convention relative to the Protection of Civilian Persons in Time of War of 12 August 1949, which have been considered by the Commission on Human Rights as war crimes and an affront to humanity, as well as its persistent defiance of the relevant resolutions of the United Nations and its continued policy of violating the basic human rights of the inhabitants of the occupied Arab territories;

2. *Reaffirms* the inalienable right of the Arab people to return to their homes and property from which they have been displaced and uprooted and calls for their return . . .;

6. *Declares* that Israel's policy of annexation, establishment of settlements and transfer of an alien population to the occupied territories is in contravention of the purposes and principles of the Charter of the United Nations, the principles and provisions of international law, the principles of sovereignty and territorial integrity and the basic human rights and fundamental freedoms of the people;

7. *Further declares* that all measures taken by Israel to change the physical character, the demographic structure and the status of occupied Arab territories are null and void;

8. *Censures* in the strongest terms all measures taken by Israel to change the status of Jerusalem.

XXII
EXCERPTS FROM RESOLUTIONS 31/106 A and C ADOPTED BY THE GENERAL ASSEMBLY ON 16 DECEMBER 1976 CONCERNING THE OCCUPIED TERRITORIES, INCLUDING JERUSALEM
A

The General Assembly,

Guided by the principles of the Charter of the United Nations, in particular the principles of sovereignty and territorial integrity,

Bearing in mind the rules of international law concerning occupation, in particular the provisions of the Geneva Convention relative to the Protection of Civilian Persons in Time of War, of 12 August 1949,[13]

1. *Strongly deplores* the measures taken by Israel in the Arab territories occupied since 1967 that alter their demographic composition or geographical nature, and particularly the establishment of settlements;

2. *Declares* that such measures have no legal validity and cannot prejudice the outcome of the search for the establishment of peace, and considers that such measures constitute an obstacle to the achievement of a just and lasting peace in the area;

3. *Declares further* that all legislative and administrative measures taken by Israel, including the expropriation of land and properties thereon and the transfer of populations, which purport to change the legal status of Jerusalem are invalid and cannot change that status;

4. *Urgently calls once more* upon Israel to rescind all those measures and to desist forthwith from taking any further measures which tend to change the demographic composition, geographical nature or status of the occupied Arab territories or any part thereof, including Jerusalem.

C

The General Assembly

6. *Reaffirms* that all measures taken by Israel to change the physical character, demographic composition, institutional structure or status of

---

13. United Nations, *Treaty Series*, vol. 75, no. 973, p. 287.

the occupied territories, or any part thereof, including Jerusalem, are null and void, and that Israel's policy of settling parts of its population and new immigrants in the occupied territories constitutes a flagrant violation of the Geneva Convention relative to the Protection of Civilian Persons in Time of War and of the relevant United Nations resolutions . . .

XXIII
EXCERPTS FROM RESOLUTION 1 (XXXIII) A ADOPTED BY THE COMMISSION ON HUMAN RIGHTS ON 15 FEBRUARY 1977 REGARDING VIOLATIONS OF HUMAN RIGHTS IN THE OCCUPIED TERRITORIES, INCLUDING JERUSALEM

A[22]

The Commission on Human Rights,

Greatly alarmed by the continuation of the violations of human rights and fundamental freedoms by Israel in the occupied Arab territories, particularly the measures aiming at annexation, as well as the continuing establishment of settlers' colonies, mass destruction of homes, torture and ill-treatment of detainees, expropriation of properties and imposition of discriminatory economic legislation,

6. *Reaffirms* that all such measures taken by Israel to change the physical character, demographic composition or status of the occupied Arab territories or any part thereof, including Jerusalem, are all null and void, and calls upon Israel to rescind all such measures already taken and to desist forthwith from taking any further action which tends to change the status of the occupied Arab territories, including Jerusalem . . .

22. Adopted at the 1390th meeting, on 15 February 1977, by a rollcall vote of 23 in favour, 3 against and 6 abstentions.

XXIV
EXCERPTS FROM RESOLUTION 32/5 ADOPTED BY THE GENERAL ASSEMBLY ON 28 OCTOBER 1977 REGARDING ILLEGAL ISRAELI MEASURES DESIGNED TO CHANGE THE LEGAL STATUS, GEOGRAPHICAL NATURE AND DEMOGRAPHIC COMPOSITION OF THE OCCUPIED TERRITORIES, INCLUDING JERUSALEM

1. *Determines* that all such measures and actions taken by Israel in the Palestinian and other Arab territories occupied since 1967 have no legal validity and constitute a serious obstruction of efforts aimed at achieving a just and lasting peace in the Middle East;

2. *Strongly deplores* the persistence of Israel in carrying out such measures, in particular the establishment of settlements in the occupied Arab territories;

3. *Calls upon* Israel to comply strictly with its international obligations in accordance with the principles of international law and the provisions of the Geneva Convention relative to the Protection of Civilian Persons in Time of War, of 12 August 1949;

4. *Calls once more upon* the Government of Israel, as the occupying Power, to desist forthwith from taking any action which would result in changing the legal status, geographical nature or demographic composition of the Arab territories occupied since 1967, including Jerusalem . . .

XXV
EXCERPTS FROM RESOLUTIONS 32/91 A AND C ADOPTED BY THE GENERAL ASSEMBLY ON 13 DECEMBER 1977 REAFFIRMING THE APPLICABILITY OF THE GENEVA CONVENTION OF 12 AUGUST 1949 TO, AND CONDEMNING ISRAELI POLICIES AND PRACTICES IN, THE OCCUPIED TERRITORIES, INCLUDING JERUSALEM

A

The General Assembly,

1. *Reaffirms* that the Geneva Convention relative to the Protection of Civilian Persons in Time of War, of 12 August 1949, is applicable to all the Arab territories occupied by Israel since 1967, including Jerusalem;

C

The General Assembly,

6. *Reaffirms* that all measures taken by Israel to change the physical character, demographic composition, institutional structure or status of the occupied territories, or any part thereof, including Jerusalem, are null and void, and that Israel's policy of settling parts of its population and new immigrants in the occupied territories constitutes a flagrant violation of the Geneva Convention relative to the Protection of Civilian Persons in Time of War and of the relevant United Nations resolutions . . .

XXVI
EXCERPTS FROM RESOLUTION OF THE GENERAL CONFERENCE OF THE UN EDUCATIONAL, SCIENTIFIC AND CULTURAL ORGANIZATION (UNESCO) OF 28 NOVEMBER 1978 CONDEMNING THE JUDAIZATION BY ISRAEL OF THE HISTORIC AND CULTURAL CONFIGURATION OF JERUSALEM

The General Conference,

Considering the exceptional importance of the cultural property in the Old City of Jerusalem, not only to the countries directly concerned but to all humanity, on account of its unique cultural, historical and religious value,

Considering that Israel, taking advantage of its military occupation of the territory, has unilaterally and in defiance of all accepted laws, taken upon itself to alter the configuration and status of the City of Jerusalem,

Considering that by resolutions 2253 (ES-V) of 4 July 1967, 2254 (ES-V) of 14 July 1967, and 32/5 of 28 October 1977, the United Nations General Assembly reaffirmed that the changes undertaken by Israel in the City of Jerusalem are unlawful, and called upon Israel to rescind all such measures already taken and to desist from taking any action which would alter the status of Jerusalem,

Considering that the United Nations Security Council noted, in resolution 252 (1968) of 21 May 1968, and in resolution 267 (1969) of 3 July 1969, that the measures taken by Israel which tend to change the status of Jerusalem are invalid and cannot change that status, and called upon Israel to rescind forthwith all measures taken by it and in future to refrain from all action likely to alter the status of Jerusalem,

Recalling that since the fifteenth session of the General Conference (1968) the Organization has urgently called on Israel to desist from any archaeological excavation in the City of Jerusalem and from any alteration of its features or its cultural and historical character, particularly with regard to Christian and Islamic religious sites (15 C/Resolutions

3.342 and 3.343, 82 EX/Decision 4.4.2, 83 EX/Decision 4.3.1, 88 EX/ Decision 4.3.1, 89 EX/Decision 4.4.1, 17 C/Resolution 3.422, 18 C/ Resolution 3.427 and 19 C/Resolution 4.129).

Condemns the Israeli occupying authorities for having infringed the resolutions adopted by the United Nations and by UNESCO, and for having continued, from the beginning of the occupation until the present, to change and Judaize the historic and cultural configuration of Jerusalem.

XXVII
EXCERPTS FROM RESOLUTIONS 33/113 A, B AND C OF THE GENERAL ASSEMBLY OF 18 DECEMBER 1978 REAFFIRMING THE NULLITY OF THE MEASURES TAKEN BY ISRAEL IN JERUSALEM

A

The General Assembly,

Recalling its resolutions 3092 A (XXVIII) of 7 December 1973, 3240 B (XXIX) of 29 November 1974, 3525 B (XXX) of 15 December 1975, 31/106 B of 16 December 1976 and 32/91 of 13 December 1977.

Considering that the Geneva Convention relative to the Protection of Civilian Persons in Time of War, of 12 August 1949, is applicable to all the Arab territories occupied since 5 June 1967,

1. *Determines* that all such measures and actions taken by Israel in the Palestinian and other Arab territories occupied since 1967 have no legal validity and constitute a serious obstruction of efforts aimed at achieving a just and lasting peace in the Middle East;

2. *Strongly deplores* the persistence of Israel in carrying out such measures, in particular the establishment of settlements in the Palestinian and other occupied Arab territories;

3. *Call upon* Israel to comply strictly with its international obligations in accordance with the principles of international law and the provisions of the Geneva Convention relative to the Protection of Civilian Persons in Time of War of 12 August 1949;

4. *Calls once more upon* the Government of Israel, as the occupying Power, to desist forthwith from taking any action which would result in changing the legal status, geographical nature or demographic composition of the Arab territories occupied since 1967, including Jerusalem;

C

The General Assembly,

6. *Reaffirms* that all measures taken by Israel to change the physical character, demographic composition, institutional structure or status of

the occupied territories, or any part thereof, including Jerusalem, are null and void, and that Israel's policy of settling parts of its population and new immigrants in the occupied territories constitutes a flagrant violation of the Geneva Convention relative to the Protection of Civilian Persons in Time of War and of the relevant United Nations resolutions.

XXVIII
EXCERPTS FROM RESOLUTION 1 (XXXV) OF THE COMMISSION ON HUMAN RIGHTS OF THE ECONOMIC AND SOCIAL COUNCIL OF THE UN DATED 21 FEBRUARY 1979 CONDEMNING ISRAEL'S VIOLATIONS OF HUMAN RIGHTS IN THE OCCUPIED TERRITORIES AND REAFFIRMING THE APPLICABILITY OF THE GENEVA CONVENTION TO SUCH TERRITORIES, INCLUDING JERUSALEM

A[37]

The Commission on Human Rights,

5. *Reaffirms* that all measures taken by Israel to change the physical character, demographic composition, institutional structure or status of the occupied territories, or any part thereof, including Jerusalem, are null and void, and that Israel's policy of settling parts of its population and new settlers in the occupied territories constitutes a flagrant violation of the Geneva Convention relative to the Protection of Civilian Persons in Time of War and of the relevant United Nations resolutions.

37. Adopted at the 1489th meeting, on 21 February 1979, by a rollcall vote by 20 votes to 2, with 9 abstentions.

XXIX
RESOLUTION 446 OF THE SECURITY COUNCIL DATED 22 MARCH 1979 CALLING UPON ISRAEL TO RESCIND MEASURES TAKEN TO CHANGE THE LEGAL STATUS, GEOGRAPHICAL NATURE AND DEMOGRAPHIC COMPOSITION OF ARAB TERRITORIES, INCLUDING JERUSALEM

The Security Council,

Having heard the statement of the permanent representative of Jordan and other statements made before the Council, stressing the urgent need to achieve a comprehensive, just and lasting peace in the Middle East, affirming once more that the Fourth Geneva Convention relative to the protection of civilian persons in time of war of 12 August 1949 is applicable to the Arab territories occupied by Israel since 1967, including Jerusalem:

1. *Determines* that the policy and practices of Israel in establishing settlements in the Palestinian and other Arab territories occupied since 1967 have no legal validity and constitute a serious obstruction to achieving a comprehensive, just and lasting peace in the Middle East.

2. *Strongly deplores* the failure of Israel to abide by Security Council Resolutions 237 (1967) of 14 June 1967, 252 (1968) of 21 May 1968 and 298 (1971) of 25 September 1971 and the Consensus Statement by the President of the Security Council on 11 November 1976 and General Assembly Resolutions 2253 E (ES-V) and 2254 (ES-V) of 4 and 14 July 1967, 32/5 of 28 October 1977 and 33/113 of 18 December 1978.

3. *Calls* once more upon Israel, as the occupying power, to abide scrupulously by the 1949 Fourth Geneva Convention, to rescind its previous measures and to desist from taking any action which would result in changing the legal status and geographical nature and materially affecting the demographic composition of the Arab territories occupied since 1967, including Jerusalem, and, in particular, not to transfer parts of its own civilian population into the occupied Arab

territories.

4. *Establishes* a commission consisting of three members of the Security Council, to be appointed by the President of the Council after consultation with the members of the Council, to examine the situation relating to settlements in the Arab territories occupied since 1967, including Jerusalem.

5. *Requests* the commission to submit its report to the Security Council by 1 July 1979.

6. *Requests* the Secretary-General to provide the commission with the necessary facilities to enable it to carry out its mission.

7. *Decides* to keep the situation in the occupied territories under constant and close scrutiny and to reconvene in July 1979 to review the situation in the light of the findings of the commission.

XXX
RESOLUTION 452 OF THE SECURITY COUNCIL DATED 20 JULY 1979 CALLING UPON ISRAEL TO CEASE THE ESTABLISHMENT OF SETTLEMENTS IN OCCUPIED TERRITORIES, INCLUDING JERUSALEM

The Security Council,

Taking note of the report and recommendations of the Security Council Commission established under resolution 446 (1979) to examine the situation relating to settlements in the Arab territories occupied since 1967, including Jerusalem, contained in document S/13450,

Strongly deploring the lack of co-operation of Israel with the Commission,

Considering that the policy of Israel in establishing settlements in the occupied Arab territories has no legal validity and constitutes a violation of the Fourth Geneva Convention relative to the Protection of Civilian Persons in Time of War of 12 August 1949,

Deeply concerned by the practices of the Israeli authorities in implementing that settlements policy in the occupied Arab territories, including Jerusalem, and its consequences for the local Arab and Palestinian population,

Emphasizing the need for confronting the issue of the existing settlements and the need to consider measures to safeguard the impartial protection of property seized,

Bearing in mind the specific status of Jerusalem, and reconfirming pertinent Security Council resolutions concerning Jerusalem and in particular the need to protect and preserve the unique spiritual and religious dimension of the Holy Places in that city,

Drawing attention to the grave consequences which the settlements policy is bound to have on any attempt to reach a peaceful solution in the Middle East,

1. *Commends* the work done by the Commission in preparing the report on the establishment of Israeli settlements in the Arab territories

occupied since 1967, including Jerusalem;

2. *Accepts* the recommendations contained in the above-mentioned report of the Commission;

3. *Calls upon* the Government and people of Israel to cease, on an urgent basis, the establishment, construction and planning of settlements in the Arab territories occupied since 1967, including Jerusalem;

4. *Requests* the Commission, in view of the magnitude of the problem of settlements, to keep under close survey the implementation of the present resolution and to report back to the Security Council before 1 November 1979.

XXXI
EXCERPTS FROM RESOLUTION 34/70 OF THE GENERAL ASSEMBLY DATED 6 DECEMBER 1979 DECLARING THAT A JUST AND LASTING SETTLEMENT MUST BE BASED ON ATTAINMENT BY THE PALESTINIAN PEOPLE OF ITS INALIENABLE RIGHTS AND ISRAELI WITHDRAWAL FROM ALL OCCUPIED TERRITORIES, INCLUDING JERUSALEM

The General Assembly,
Having discussed the item entitled 'The situation in the Middle East',

Deeply concerned that the Arab territories occupied since 1967 have continued, for more than twelve years, to be under illegal Israeli occupation and that the Palestinian people, after three decades, is still deprived of the exercise of its inalienable national rights,

Reaffirming that the acquisition of territory by force is inadmissible under the Charter of the United Nations and that all territories thus occupied must be returned,

Reaffirming also the urgent necessity of the establishment of a just, comprehensive and lasting peace in the region, based on full respect for the principles of the Charter of the United Nations as well as for its resolutions concerning the situation in the Middle East and the question of Palestine,

Convinced that the early convening of the Peace Conference on the Middle East with the participation of all parties concerned, including the Palestine Liberation Organization, in accordance with relevant resolutions of the General Assembly, particularly resolution 3375 (XXX) of 10 November 1975, is essential for the realization of a just and lasting settlement in the region,

1. *Condemns* Israel's continued occupation of Palestinian and other Arab territories, in violation of the Charter of the United Nations, the principles of international law and relevant resolutions of the United Nations;

2. *Declares once more* that peace is indivisible and that a just and lasting settlement of the Middle East question must be based on a comprehensive solution, under the auspices of the United Nations, which takes into account all aspects of the Arab-Israeli conflict, in particular the attainment by the Palestinian people of all its inalienable rights and the Israeli withdrawal from all the occupied Arab and Palestinian territories, including Jerusalem;

3. *Condemns* all partial agreements and separate treaties which violate the recognized rights of the Palestinian people and contradict the principles of just and comprehensive solutions to the Middle East problem to ensure the establishment of a just peace in the area;

4. *Reaffirms* that until Israel, in accordance with relevant resolutions of the United Nations, withdraws from all the occupied Palestinian and other Arab territories, and until the Palestinian people attains and exercises its inalienable right, as affirmed by the General Assembly in resolution 3236 (XXIX) of 22 November 1974, a comprehensive, just and lasting peace in the Middle East, in which all countries and peoples in the region live in peace and security within recognized and secure boundaries, will not be achieved;

5. *Calls anew* for the early convening of the Peace Conference on the Middle East, under the auspices of the United Nations and the co-chairmanship of the Union of Soviet Socialist Republics and the United States of America, with the participation on an equal footing of all parties concerned, including the Palestine Liberation Organization in accordance with General Assembly resolution 3375 (XXX);

6. *Urges* the parties to the conflict and all other interested parties to work towards the achievement of a comprehensive settlement covering all aspects of the problem and worked out with the participation of all parties concerned within the framework of the United Nations;

7. *Requests* the Security Council, in the exercise of its responsibilities under the Charter, to take all necessary measures in order to ensure the implementation of relevant resolutions of both the Security Council and the General Assembly, including Assembly resolution 34/65 A and the present resolution, and to facilitate the achievement of such a comprehensive settlement aiming at the establishment of a just and lasting peace in the region.

XXXII
EXCERPTS FROM RESOLUTIONS 1 A AND B (XXXVI) OF THE COMMISSION ON HUMAN RIGHTS OF THE ECONOMIC AND SOCIAL COUNCIL OF THE UN DATED 13 FEBRUARY 1980 ON THE VIOLATIONS OF HUMAN RIGHTS IN THE OCCUPIED TERRITORIES, INCLUDING JERUSALEM

A[1]

The Commission on Human Rights,

Guided by the purposes and principles of the Charter of the United Nations as well as the principles and provisions of the Universal Declaration of Human Rights,

Bearing in mind the provisions of the Geneva Convention relative to the Protection of Civilian Persons in Time of War of 12 August 1949 and of other relevant conventions and regulations,

Reaffirming the fact that occupation itself constitutes a fundamental violation of the human rights of the civilian population of the occupied Arab territories;

1. *Calls upon Israel* to take immediate steps for the return of the Palestinians and the other displaced inhabitants of the occupied Arab territories to their homes and property;

2. *Declares* that Israel's grave breaches of the Geneva Convention relative to the Protection of Civilian Persons in Time of War of 12 August 1949 are war crimes and an affront to humanity;

3. *Condemns* the following Israeli policies and practices:

(*a*) The annexation of parts of the occupied territories;

(*b*) The establishment of Israeli settlements therein and the transfer of an alien population thereto;

---

1. Adopted at the 1538th meeting, on 13 February 1980, by a rollcall vote of 28 in favour, 3 against and 8 abstentions.

(*c*) The evacuation, deportation, expulsion, displacement and transfer of Arab inhabitants of the occupied territories, and the denial of their right to return;

(*d*) The confiscation and expropriation of Arab property in the occupied territories and all other transactions for the acquisition of land involving Israeli authorities, institutions or nationals on the one hand, and inhabitants or institutions of the occupied territories on the other and most recently the expropriation of the Arab electric company of Jerusalem;

(*e*) The destruction and demolition of Arab houses;

(*f*) Mass arrests, administrative detention and ill-treatment of the Arab population and the torture of persons under detention;

(*g*) The pillaging of archaeological and cultural property;

(*h*) The interference with religious freedoms and practices as well as with family rights and customs;

(*i*) The continuous interference with and obstruction of the educational scholastic activities and the brutal suppression of all forms of students' opinion, expression and manifestation;

(*j*) The illegal exploitation of the natural wealth, resources and population of the occupied territories;

(*k*) The arming of the settlers in occupied territories to commit acts of violence against the Arab civilians;

4. *Further condemns* administrative and legislative measures by the Israeli authorities to encourage, promote and expand the establishment of settlers' colonies in the occupied territories, which further demonstrate Israel's determination to annex those territories;

5. *Reaffirms* that all measures taken by Israel to change the physical character, demographic composition, institutional structure or status of the occupied territories, or any part thereof, including Jerusalem, are null and void, and that Israel's policy of settling parts of its population and new settlers in the occupied territories constitutes a flagrant violation of the Geneva Convention relative to the Protection of Civilian Persons in Time of War and of the relevant United Nations resolutions;

6. *Demands* that Israel desist forthwith from the policies and practices referred to in paragraphs 3, 4 and 5 above;

7. *Demands* that Israel cease forthwith all acts of torture and ill-treatment of Arab detainees and prisoners;

8. *Calls upon* Israel to release all Arabs detained or imprisoned as a result of their struggle for self-determination and the liberation of their territories, and to accord to them, pending their release, the protection envisaged in the relevant provisions of the international instruments

concerning the treatment of prisoners of war;

B²

The Commission on Human Rights,

Recognizing that the failure of Israel to apply the Geneva Convention relative to the Protection of Civilian Persons in Time of War of 12 August 1949, poses a grave threat to world peace and security;

Taking into account that States parties to the Geneva Convention of 12 August 1949 undertake, in accordance with article 1 thereof, not only to respect but also to ensure respect for the Conventions in all circumstances;

1. *Expresses its deep concern* at the consequences of Israel's refusal to apply fully and effectively the Geneva Convention relative to the Protection of Civilian Persons in Time of War in all its provisions to all the Arab territories occupied since 1967, including Jerusalem;

2. *Reaffirms* that the Geneva Convention relative to the Protection of Civilian Persons in Time of War is applicable to all the Arab territories occupied by Israel since 1967, including Jerusalem;

3. *Condemns* the failure of Israel to acknowledge the applicability of that Convention to the territories it has occupied since 1967, including Jerusalem;

4. *Calls upon* Israel to abide by and respect the obligations arising from the Charter of the United Nations and other instruments and rules of international law, in particular the provisions of the Geneva Convention relative to the Protection of Civilian Persons in Time of War, in all the Arab territories occupied since 1967, including Jerusalem;

XXXIII
RESOLUTION 465 OF THE SECURITY COUNCIL DATED 1 MARCH 1980 CALLING UPON ISRAEL TO CEASE THE ESTABLISHMENT OF SETTLEMENTS AND TO DISMANTLE EXISTING SETTLEMENTS IN OCCUPIED TERRITORIES, INCLUDING JERUSALEM

The Security Council,

Taking note of the reports of the Commission of the Security Council established under resolution 446 (1979) to examine the situation relating to settlements in the Arab territories occupied since 1967, including Jerusalem, contained in documents S/13450 and Corr. 1 and S/13679,

Taking note also of letters from the Permanent Representative of Jordan (S/13801) and the Permanent Representative of Morocco, Chairman of the Islamic Group (S/13802),

Strongly deploring the refusal by Israel to co-operate with the Commission and regretting its formal rejection of resolutions 446 (1979) and 452 (1979),

Affirming once more that the Fourth Geneva Convention relative to the Protection of Civilian Persons in Time of War of 12 August 1949 is applicable to the Arab territories occupied by Israel since 1967, including Jerusalem,

Deploring the decision of the Government of Israel to officially support Israeli settlement in the Palestinian and other Arab territories occupied since 1967,

Deeply concerned over the practices of the Israeli authorities in inplementing that settlement policy in the occupied Arab territories, including Jerusalem, and its consequences for the local Arab and Palestinian population,

Taking into account the need to consider measures for the impartial protection of private and public land and property, and water resources,

Bearing in mind the specific status of Jerusalem and, in particular, the need for protection and preservation of the unique spiritual and religious dimension of the Holy Places in the city,

Drawing attention to the grave consequences which the settlement policy is bound to have on any attempt to reach a comprehensive, just and lasting peace in the Middle East,

Recalling pertinent Security Council resolutions, specifically resolutions 237 (1967) of 14 June 1967, 252 (1968) of 21 May 1968, 267 (1969) of 3 July 1969, 271 (1969) of 15 September 1969 and 298 (1971) of 25 September 1971, as well as the consensus statement made by the President of the Security Council on 11 November 1976,

Having invited Mr. Fahd Qawasmeh, Mayor of Al-Khalil (Hebron), in the occupied territory, to supply it with information pursuant to rule 39 of the provisional rules of procedure,

1. *Commends* the work done by the Commission in preparing the report contained in document S/13679;

2. *Accepts* the conclusions and recommendations contained in the above-mentioned report of the Commission;

3. *Calls upon* all parties, particularly the Government of Israel, to co-operate with the Commission;

4. *Strongly deplores* the decision of Israel to prohibit the free travel of Mayor Fahd Qawasmeh in order to appear before the Security Council, and requests Israel to permit his free travel to the United Nations Headquarters for that purpose;

5. *Determines* that all measures taken by Israel to change the physical character, demographic composition, institutional structure or status of the Palestinian and other Arab territories occupied since 1967, including Jerusalem, or any part thereof, have no legal validity and that Israel's policy and practices of settling parts of its population and new immigrants in those territories constitute a flagrant violation of the Fourth Geneva Convention relative to the Protection of Civilian Persons in Time of War and also constitute a serious obstruction to achieving a comprehensive, just and lasting peace in the Middle East;

6. *Strongly deplores* the continuation and persistence of Israel in pursuing those policies and practices and calls upon the Government and people of Israel to rescind those measures, to dismantle the existing settlements and in particular to cease, on an urgent basis, the establishment, construction and planning of settlements in the Arab territories occupied since 1967, including Jerusalem;

7. *Calls upon* all States not to provide Israel with any assistance to be used specifically in connexion with settlements in the occupied territories;

8. *Requests* the Commission to continue to examine the situation relating to settlements in the Arab territories occupied since 1967, including Jerusalem, to investigate the reported serious depletion of natural resources, particularly the water resources, with a view to ensuring the protection of those important natural resources of the territories under occupation, and to keep under close scrutiny the implementation of the present resolution;

9. *Requests* the Commission to report to the Security Council before 1 September 1980, and decides to convene at the earliest possible date thereafter in order to consider the report and the full implementation of the present resolution.

XXXIV
RESOLUTION 476 (1980) ADOPTED BY THE SECURITY COUNCIL ON 30 JUNE 1980 RECONFIRMING THAT ALL LEGISLATIVE AND ADMINISTRATIVE MEASURES TAKEN BY ISRAEL WHICH PURPORT TO ALTER THE CHARACTER AND STATUS OF THE HOLY CITY OF JERUSALEM HAVE NO LEGAL VALIDITY

The Security Council,

Having considered the letter of 28 May 1980 from the representative of Pakistan, the current Chairman of the Organization of the Islamic Conference, as contained in document S/13966 of 28 May 1980,

Reaffirming that acquisition of territory by force is inadmissible,

Bearing in mind the specific status of Jerusalem and, in particular, the need for protection and preservation of the unique spiritual and religious dimension of the Holy Places in the city,

Reaffirming its resolutions relevant to the character and status of the Holy City of Jerusalem, in particular resolutions 252 (1968) of 21 May 1968, 267 (1969) of 3 July 1969, 271 (1969) of 15 September 1969, 298 (1971) of 25 September 1971 and 465 (1980) of 1 March 1980,

Recalling the Fourth Geneva Convention of 12 August 1949 relative to the Protection of Civilian Persons in Time of War,

Deploring the persistence of Israel in changing the physical character, demographic composition, institutional structure and the status of the Holy City of Jerusalem,

Gravely concerned over the legislative steps initiated in the Israeli Knesset with the aim of changing the character and status of the Holy City of Jerusalem,

1. *Reaffirms* the overriding necessity to end the prolonged occupation of Arab territories occupied by Israel since 1967, including Jerusalem;

2. *Strongly deplores* the continued refusal of Israel, the occupying Power, to comply with the relevant resolutions of the Security Council

and the General Assembly;

3. *Reconfirms* that all legislative and administrative measures and actions taken by Israel, the occupying Power, which purport to alter the character and status of the Holy City of Jerusalem have no legal validity and constitute a flagrant violation of the Fourth Geneva Convention relative to the Protection of Civilian Persons in Time of War and also constitute a serious obstruction to achieving a comprehensive, just and lasting peace in the Middle East;

4. *Reiterates* that all such measures which have altered the geographic, demographic and historical character and status of the Holy City of Jerusalem are null and void and must be rescinded in compliance with the relevant resolutions of the Security Council;

5. *Urgently calls* on Israel, the occupying Power, to abide by this and previous Security Council resolutions and to desist forthwith from persisting in the policy and measures affecting the character and status of the Holy City of Jerusalem;

6. *Reaffirms* its determination in the event of non-compliance by Israel with this resolution, to examine practical ways and means in accordance with relevant provisions of the Charter of the United Nations to secure the full implementation of this resolution.

XXXV
RESOLUTION ES/72/ (1980) ADOPTED BY THE GENERAL ASSEMBLY ON 29 JULY 1980 REQUIRING ISRAEL TO WITHDRAW FROM ALL TERRITORIES OCCUPIED IN 1967, INCLUDING JERUSALEM

The General Assembly,

Having considered the question of Palestine at an emergency special session,

Convinced that the failure to solve this question poses a grave threat to international peace and security,

Noting with regret and concern that the Security Council, at its 2220th meeting on 30 April 1980, failed to take a decision, as a result of the negative vote of the United States of America, on the recommendation of the Committee on the Exercise of the Inalienable Rights of the Palestinian People endorsed by the General Assembly in its resolutions 31/20 of 24 November 1976, 32/40A of 2 December 1977, 33/28A of 7 December 1978 and 34/65A of 29 November 1979,

Having considered the letter dated 1 July 1980 of the Permanent Representative of Senegal, Chairman of the Committee on the Exercise of the Inalienable Rights of the Palestinian People,

Having heard the statement by the Observer of the Palestine Liberation Organization, the representative of the Palestinian people,

1. *Recalls and reaffirms* its resolutions 3236 (XXIX) and 3237 (XXIX) of 22 November 1974 and all other relevant resolutions pertinent to the question of Palestine;

2. *Reaffirms*, in particular, that a comprehensive, just and lasting peace in the Middle East cannot be established in accordance with the Charter of the United Nations and the relevant United Nations resolutions, without the withdrawal of Israel from all the occupied Palestinian and other Arab territories, including Jerusalem, and without the achievement of a just solution of the problem of Palestine on the basis of the attainment of the inalienable rights of the Palestinian people in

Palestine;

3. *Reaffirms* the inalienable right of the Palestinians to return to their homes and property, in Palestine, from which they have been displaced and uprooted and calls for their return;

4. *Reaffirms* the inalienable rights in Palestine of the Palestinian people, including:

(*a*) The right to self-determination without external interference and to national independence and sovereignty;

(*b*) The right to establish its own independent sovereign state;

5. *Reaffirms* the right of the Palestine Liberation Organization, the representative of the Palestinian people, to participate on an equal footing in all efforts, deliberations and conferences on the question of Palestine and the situation in the Middle East within the framework of the United Nations;

6. *Reaffirms* the fundamental principle of the inadmissibility of the acquisition of territory by force;

7. *Calls upon* Israel to withdraw completely and unconditionally from all the Palestinian and other Arab territories occupied since June 1967, including Jerusalem, with all property and services intact, and urges that such withdrawal from all the occupied territories should start before 15 November 1980;

8. *Demands* that Israel should fully comply with the provisions of Resolution 465 (1980) adopted unanimously by the Security Council on 1 March 1980;

9. *Further demands* that Israel should fully comply with all United Nations resolutions relevant to the historic character of the Holy City of Jerusalem, in particular Security Council Resolution 476 of 30 June 1980;

10. *Expresses* its opposition to all policies and plans aimed at the resettlement of the Palestinians outside their homeland;

11. *Requests and authorizes* the Secretary General, in consultation, as appropriate, with the Committee on the Exercise of the Inalienable Rights of the Palestinian People, to take the necessary measures towards the implementation of the recommendations contained in paragraphs 59 to 72 of the report of the Committee to the General Assembly at its thirty-first session as a basis for the solution of the question of Palestine;

12. *Requests* the Secretary General to report to the General Assembly at its thirty-fifth session on the implementation of the present resolution;

13. *Requests* the Security Council, in the event of noncompliance by

Israel with the present resolution, to convene in order to consider the situation and the adoption of effective measures under Chapter VII of the Charter;

14. *Decides* to adjourn the seventh emergency special session temporarily and to authorize the president of the latest regular session of the General Assembly to resume its meetings upon request from member states.

XXXVI
RESOLUTION 478 ADOPTED BY THE SECURITY COUNCIL ON 20 AUGUST 1980 WHICH CENSURED THE ENACTMENT BY ISRAEL OF A BASIC LAW PROCLAIMING A CHANGE IN THE CHARACTER AND STATUS OF JERUSALEM AND DECLARED IT NULL AND VOID

The Security Council,

Recalling its resolution 476 (1980) of 30 June 1980,

Reaffirming again that the acquisition of territory by force is inadmissible,

Deeply concerned over the enactment of a 'basic law' in the Israeli Knesset proclaiming a change in the character and status of the Holy City of Jerusalem, with its implications for peace and security,

Noting that Israel has not complied with Security Council resolution 476 (1980),

Reaffirming its determination to examine practical ways and means, in accordance with the relevant provisions of the Charter of the United Nations, to secure the full implementation of its resolution 476 (1980), in the event of non-compliance by Israel,

1. *Censures* in the strongest terms the enactment by Israel of the 'basic law' on Jerusalem and the refusal to comply with relevant Security Council resolutions;

2. *Affirms* that the enactment of the 'basic law' by Israel constitutes a violation of international law and does not affect the continued application of the Fourth Geneva Convention of 12 August 1949 Relative to the Protection of Civilian Persons in Time of War in the Palestinian and other Arab territories occupied since June 1967, including Jerusalem;

3. *Determines* that all legislative and administrative measures and actions taken by Israel, the occupying Power, which have altered or purport to alter the character and status of the Holy City of Jerusalem, and, in particular, the recent 'basic law' on Jerusalem, are null and void

and must be rescinded forthwith;

4. *Affirms also* that this action constitutes a serious obstruction to achieving a comprehensive, just and lasting peace in the Middle East;

5. *Decides* not to recognize the 'basic law' and such other actions by Israel that, as a result of this law, seek to alter the character and status of Jerusalem and calls upon all Members of the United Nations:

(a) to accept this decision;

(b) and upon those States that have established diplomatic Missions in Jerusalem to withdraw such Missions from the Holy City;

6. *Requests* the Secretary-General to report to the Security Council on the implementation of this resolution before 15 November 1980;

7. *Decides* to remain seized of this serious situation.

POSTSCRIPT

While this book was in the press certain important developments occurred in respect of Jerusalem.

In reaction to a bill submitted to the Israeli Knesset, proposing to proclaim an undivided Jerusalem the eternal capital of Israel, the Security Council adopted on 30 June 1980, by 14 to 0, with the US abstaining, Resolution 476 which reaffirmed the necessity to end Israel's occupation of Jerusalem and other Arab territory and reconfirmed the invalidity of all legislative and administrative measures it has taken to alter the character and status of the Holy City (Appendix XXXIV).

Then on 29 July the General Assembly adopted in an emergency special session by a vote of 112 to 7 with 24 abstentions Resolution ES-7/2 which called upon Israel to withdraw completely and unconditionally from all territories occupied in 1967, including Jerusalem, and urged that such withdrawal should start before 15 November 1980. The Resolution further requested the Security Council, in the event of Israel's non-compliance, to consider the situation and the adoption of effective measures under Chapter VII of the Charter (Appendix XXXV).

Undeterred by a long line of UN resolutions, including the last Resolution of the General Assembly which it rejected as being 'illegal' — a strange argument coming from a state steeped in illegality — Israel enacted on the following day a so-called 'basic law' which proclaimed Jerusalem its eternal capital.

This act of folly aroused the wrath of the Arab and Islamic world and was universally condemned by the international community. Iraq and Saudi Arabia, the Middle East's largest oil exporters, announced on 6 August that they will break off diplomatic and economic relations with any country which may recognize Jerusalem as Israel's capital and called on governments which had embassies there to withdraw them from the city. This decision was adopted on 20 August by the Committee of *Al-Qods* (Jerusalem) acting on behalf of Arab and Islamic States which form the Organization of Islamic States.

Israel's action was also censured in the strongest terms by the Security Council on 20 August 1980 in Resolution 478 which was adopted by 14 votes to 0 with the US abstaining (Appendix XXXVI). The Council declared that the enactment of the 'basic law' on Jerusalem by Israel was a violation of international law and that all legislative and administrative measures and actions taken by Israel, the occupying power, which have altered or purport to alter the character and status of the Holy City of Jerusalem, and, in particular, the recent basic law, are null and void and must be rescinded forthwith. The Council further called upon those States that have established diplomatic missions in Jerusalem to withdraw them from the Holy City.

The US abstained from this last Resolution under the pretext advanced by its Secretary of State, Mr Edward Muskie, that it was 'unbalanced and unrealistic'. Such explanation convinces no one and can only be ascribed to a desire to placate Israel and woo Jewish voters in the presidential election. It is hard to understand how a resolution of the Security Council which condemns a grave violation of international law and UN resolutions and declares void a blatant usurpation of the Holy City by the occupying power could be considered to be 'unbalanced'. One also fails to understand why such a resolution should be considered 'unrealistic' unless, of course, the intention is to condone the wrong. The US abstention in this case is not conducive to peace since it suggests indifference to, if not acquiescence in, Israel's usurpation of Jerusalem. The irony of the matter is that such abstention did not satisfy Israel which rebuked the Carter administration for not using its veto. Israel was all the more irritated since it was encouraged to believe by the declarations of support made by some presidential candidates for the proclamation of Jerusalem as its capital.

The usurpation of Jerusalem is not rendered any less reprehensible by the assurance given by Israel that it would not prevent access by the adherents of all faiths to their Holy Places. The *Osservatore Romano* of 30 June-1 July 1980 which usually reflects the Vatican's view wrote that the question of Jerusalem 'cannot be reduced simply to one of free access to the Holy Places' because its universal character and its significance to three religions are such that they place it beyond the interests of a single state and require that it be subject to 'an appropriate juridical system which is guaranteed by a high international authority'.

As a result of the call made by the Security Council for the withdrawal of foreign diplomatic missions from Jerusalem and the warning made by the Arab States in this regard, eleven out of the thirteen states which maintained embassies in Jerusalem moved them to Tel-Aviv. These were Venezuela, Uruguay, the Netherlands, Chile, Ecuador,

Salvador, Costa Rica, Haiti, Panama, Colombia and Bolivia. At the time of writing, only two had not made up their mind, namely, Guatemala and the Dominican Republic.

By proclaiming Jerusalem its capital, Israel has played with fire and transformed the Arab-Israeli conflict from a political into a highly emotional and religious struggle between three million Israelis and seven hundred million Arabs and Moslems, not to speak of the strong provocation caused to the feelings of the Christian world. In this regard, it should be emphasized that the conflict is with the Israelis and not with the Jews generally because the present explosive situation has been created not by Judaism, which is one of the three great religions, but by Zionism which has exploited religion for political and territorial aggression.

Following Israel's adoption of its law on Jerusalem, Prince Fahd, Crown Prince of Saudi Arabia, referred to the possibility of a holy war (*jihad*) over Jerusalem and Saddam Hussein, the Iraqi President, is reported to have said that dropping bombs on Tel-Aviv would be a more effective remedy to stem Israeli expansionism than the severance of relations with countries which recognize Israel's action in Jerusalem.

Still more important decisions to combat Israel's action were taken by the Conference of 43 Arab and Islamic Foreign Ministers at Fez on 20 September 1980. These decisions define the concrete measures to be taken for the liberation of Jerusalem and the recovery by the people of Palestine of its inalienable rights.

Regarding Jerusalem, the Conference decided, *inter alia*

(a) to reaffirm the undertaking of Islamic States to use their political, financial, petroleum and military potentialities to face Israel's annexation of Jerusalem and their determination to apply a political and economic boycott against countries which subscribe to Israel's decision, or collaborate in its execution or establish diplomatic missions in Jerusalem (Decision 2);

(b) to request the General Assembly of the UN to reject the credentials of the Israeli delegation to the UN since it represents a government which violates international law in making Jerusalem its capital (Decision 15);

(c) to proclaim the total adherence of Islamic States to *Jihad* (holy war) with the vast implications of a human character which it entails, and with the knowledge that it involves a struggle against the Zionist enemy in all fields: military, political, economic, cultural and informational (Decision 23).

The decision to seek Israel's exclusion from the General Assembly of the UN, just as happened to South Africa by reason of its apartheid policy, immediately caused President Carter in an election speech in New York to threaten that, in the event of Israel's exclusion, the US would have to reconsider its attitude towards the General Assembly. In other words, this means that the US might be prepared, for the sake of supporting Israel's action in Jerusalem, to destroy the very structure of the UN.

The reactions of the Arab and Islamic world give a measure of the deep emotions which have been aroused by Israel's provocative action and suggest that, in addition to other international repercussions, the new situation created in Jerusalem could well become the detonator of one of the bloodiest conflicts in history in comparison with which the Crusades pale into insignificance.

The worst can yet be averted by effective coercive measures by the international community to subdue Israel's blatant defiance of its will and force it to respect the legal status of Jerusalem and withdraw from the city. It is futile, however, to imagine that Israel would do so, without recourse by the international community to force or extreme pressure. Since its creation Israel, flouting UN resolutions and trampling upon the principles of international law, has made the *fait accompli*, regardless of its illegality or wrongfulness, the criterion of its actions. It has been encouraged in such conduct by the fact that it was never checked or restrained save once following its Suez aggression in 1956. The UN cannot continue to deal with the problem of Jerusalem as it has done in the past simply by verbal condemnations or the adoption of new resolutions. There is no dearth of condemnations and resolutions. What is needed is not resolutions, but only resolution in their implementation. With the American presidential election over, one ventures to hope that the US will have the wisdom to see where its duty and also its interest lie and will abandon its patronage of Israel so as to enable the taking of effective international action for the preservation of humanity's precious and unique heritage in the Holy City of Jerusalem.

INDEX

Abdullah, King 58, 131, 132
Abraham 19, 22
Absentee Property Law and
  Regulations 63
Abu Dis 104, 164
Ad Hoc Committee on Palestine 56,
  58, 59, 61, 72, 131
Advisory Council for Palestine 146
Aelia Capitolina 24
Afghanistan 148, 150
Al-Aqsa Mosque 11, 27, 74, 75,
  124, 144, 157
Alexander the Great 23
Allenby, General 29
Allon, Ygal 20
Amman 64
Arab Higher Committee 47
Arab-Israeli War, 1967 69
Arab Legion of Jordan 46, 49, 50-1
Arab rule in Palestine 26-7, 29,
  155, 156
Arab States, League of 64
Armistice Agreement, 1949 51
Ascension, Church of the 25, 130
Assyrians 23, 155
Azcarate, Pablo de 46-7

Bab El Zahreh 132
Babylonians 12, 23, 43, 93, 155
Bakaa, Lower and Upper 51, 132
Balfour Declaration 14, 29, 34, 35,
  46
Ball, George W. 150
Bar-Kochba revolt 24
Beersheba 50
Begin, Menachem 37, 115, 150
Beit Jala 72
Beit Sahur 72
Ben Gurion, David 48, 150
Benjamin of Tudela 95
Benjamites 20, 22
Bernadotte, Count 40, 51, 55, 62
Bethany 131, 157
Bethlehem 24, 28, 50, 72, 104, 131,
  157, 164
Bible, the 21
Bridgeman, Rev. Charles T. 45
Britain *see following entry and*

United Kingdom
British Mandate in Palestine 33-40,
  103-4, 107, 132, 146, 160-1;
  Jewish immigration during 12, 34,
  35, 36, 37
Buber, Martin 13
Bull, General Odd 69
Buraq, Al 157
Byzantium 24, 25, 27

Camp David 115, 116
Canaanites 19-21, 94, 155
Capitulations, the 28
Carter, President Jimmy 85-7, 115,
  139-40, 149
Cenacle 11, 74-5, 130, 157
Charlemagne, Emperor 25
Chosroes II, King 25
Christian rule in Jerusalem 24-6,
  155, 156
Christians in Jerusalem 11, 26, 27, 28,
  74-5, 97
Commission on Jewish settlements in
  occupied territories 82
Committee on the Exercise of the
  Inalienable Rights of the
  Palestinians 109, 217
Conciliation Commission 56, 62, 63,
  122-3, 171
Conference of Islamic States 112
Constantine, Emperor 24, 25, 95
Consular Truce Commission 46
Crimean War 28
Crusades 26
Cyrus, King 23

David, King 19, 20, 21, 22, 23, 93,
  94; Tomb of 157
Dayan, Moshe 71
Deir Abu Tor 49, 51, 132
Deir Yassin 44, 50, 81
Dome of the Rock, Mosque of the
  11, 27, 157
Dulles, John Foster 110-11

Eban, Abba 59-60, 72, 107
Egypt 20, 21, 23, 27, 50, 69, 93, 155;
  Peace Treaty with Israel 114-16, 145

225

Ein Karem 81, 104, 131, 157, 164
Eisenhower, President Dwight D. 140
Elon Moreh 87
Eshkol, Levi 71
Eytan, Walter 57

Ferdinand, King of Spain 94
First World War 28
France 28
Francois I 28
Frederick II, Emperor 26

Galilee 24, 25
Garden Tomb 130, 157
Gaza 50, 138
Gaza Strip 69
General Assembly Resolutions on
    Jerusalem and Palestine:
    181 59, 61, 81, 87, 88, 98, 105,
    106-8, 109, 110, 115, 117, 145,
    147, 160-9; 194 56, 57, 58, 59,
    61, 62, 87, 105, 108, 171-4; 242
    116, 129-31, 132, 138, 180-1,
    303 56, 57, 87, 105,
    108, 176-7; 394 63; 2252 70;
    2253 83, 109, 123, 138, 178;
    2254 83, 123, 138, 179; 2851
    138, 189; 3236 123; 3376 109;
    31/106 192-3; 32/5 83, 138,
    195; 32/91 196; 33/113 83,
    138-9, 199-200; 34/70 206-7;
    ES/72 216-18; *for resolutions
    listed by subject, see* United
    Nations Resolutions on Jerusalem
    and Palestine
Geneva Convention, Fourth 83, 84,
    87, 122, 125, 138, 185, 196, 201,
    208, 210, 211, 212, 215
Germany 28
Gethsemane, Garden of 11, 130, 157
Gilboa, battle of 21
Ginsberg, Asher 13
Glubb, John Bagot 46, 49
Godefroi de Bouillon 26
Golan region 69, 138
Goldberg, Arthur 112, 115
Goldmann, Nahum 149-50
Golgotha, Church of the 25
Greece 23, 93, 155
Gush Emunim 87
Gussing, N.G. 70

Haam, Ahad 13
Hadawi, Sami 98
Hadrian, Emperor 12, 24, 25, 95

Haganah 37, 49, 50
Hakem Bi Amr Illah 25
Haram Al-Sharif 11, 27, 36, 73, 74,
    75, 76, 98, 157
Harun Al Rashid, Caliph 25
Hassan Bin Talal 105
Hebron 13, 21, 50, 73, 84, 86
Helena, Empress 25
Heraclius, Emperor 25, 95
Herod, King 12, 24
Herzl, Theodor 13, 93
Hinnom, vale of 49
Holy Places 11-12, 28, 40, 56, 58,
    73-5, 98-9, 114, 125, 144, 145,
    157; *see also under names of
    and under* United Nations
    Resolutions on Jerusalem and
    Palestine
Holy Sepulchre 11; Church of the
    25, 26, 75, 157
Human Rights, Commission on 123,
    125-6, 190, 191, 194, 201,
    208-10
Hussein, King 69

Ibrahimi Mosque 73
International Court of Justice 143,
    148-9
Iran 148, 149
Iraq 33, 34
Irgun Zvai Leumi 37, 44, 50
Israel: assurances to UN 58-61, 72;
    establishment of the State 12, 14,
    39, 46; Jewish immigration into
    62-3, *see also under* British
    Mandate, Jerusalem *and* Palestine;
    judaization of 197-8; Peace
    Treaty with Egypt 114-16, 145;
    sanctions against proposed 139-40,
    143; UN, admission to 58-9, 60,
    61, 107, 175
Israelis, racial identity 94
Israelites 19, 21-2, 94, 155

Jaffa 48
Jaffa Gate 49
Japho 21
Jarring mission 150
Jebusites 20, 21, 22
Jericho 49, 70
Jerusalem: Arab property and land
    confiscated 63, 81, 82-3, 97-8,
    121-2, 124; Arabs displaced from
    45, 70, 81, 83; battle for 43-51;
    capital of Israel *see* Postscript;

capital status of 34, 61, 115;
conservatory measures suggested
144-8; *corpus separatum* 38, 44,
45, 46, 56, 57, 72, 82, 89, 96,
104, 116, 117, 129, 130, 164,
170, 176; de-Christianization
of 97; demographical data on 45,
57, 61-3, 70-1, 81, 95, 117, 121,
122, 125, 144; destruction of
important sites in 75-7; embassies, withdrawal of *see* Postscript;
history of to 1917 19-29, 95-6;
internationalization of 14, 37-8,
46, 50, 55-8, 60, 63, 87, 104-8,
109, 113, 116-17, *see also under*
United Nations Resolutions on
Jerusalem and Palestine; Jewish
immigration into 62, 81-9, 117,
125; Jews deported from and
prohibited in 12, 24; judaization
of 62, 71, 82, 93-4, 197-8, *see
also* Jerusalem, Jewish immigration
into; Latin Kingdom of 26; legal
aspects of Israel's activities 121-2;
legal status of 103-17; maps of
158, 170; New town annexed by
Israel 61; New town seized by
Israel 45-8; Old city annexed by
Israel 69-77; Old city attacked by
Israelis, 1948 49-51; Old city
incorporated into Jordan 64, 111;
partition proposal 131-3; religious
significance of 11-12, 130-1, *see
also* Holy Places; settlements in
87
Jesus Christ 24-5, 28, 157
Jewish rule in Jerusalem 21-3
John Paul II, Pope 113
John the Baptist 131
Jordan 33-4, 49-51, 55-6, 58, 63-4,
69, 70, 73, 132, 211
Josephus 19
Judah 22, 93
Judaism 11-12
Judea 24
Julian the Apostate 95

Kalandia airport 72
Katamon 46, 47, 51, 132
Kennedy, Senator Edward 86
Kenyon, Kathleen 20, 23, 43
King-Crane Commission 98-9
King David Hotel 37
Kissinger, Dr Henry 140, 148
Knesset 61, 86, 114, 115

Lausanne, Treaty of 103
League of Arab States 64
League of Nations 14; Article 22 of
Covenant 33-4, 103-4, 107
Lebanon 33, 34
Levin, Harry 49
Lifta 81
Looting 48

Maccabaeus, Simon 23
Maccabees 23, 93
Macedonians 12
Maheu, René 76
Malek, Caliph Abdul 27
Malha, El 81
Mamillah 51, 132; Cemetery 75, 131
Mandate *see* British Mandate
Melchisedek, priest of 'El Elyon 19,
22
Mesopotamia 21
Milk Grotto 131
Mohamed Ali 27
Moriah, Mount 22
Mosque of Al-Aqsa *see under* Al-Aqsa
Mosque of the Dome of the Rock 11,
27, 73, 157
Moslem rule in Jerusalem 24, 25,
26-9
Mughrabi quarter 75
Musrarah 48, 51, 132

Nahman, Moise Ben 95
National Council of Churches 113-14
Nativity, Church of the 11, 25, 28,
131
Nazareth 24, 25, 172
Nebi Daoud 51, 132
Nebuchadnezzar, King 23

Occupied territories 83-7; settlements
in 125, 190; *see also under* United
Nations Resolutions on Jerusalem
and Palestine
Oil 149, 150
Olives, Mount of 11, 25, 130, 157
Omar, Mosque of 73
Omar Ibn Al Khattab, Caliph 26, 114
Omari Mosque 27
Organization of the Islamic Confer-
ence 112-13

Palestine: Arab land seized by Israelis
86; Arab revolt, 1936-9 35; Arabs
displaced from 43-4, *see also
under* Jerusalem; history of to

1917 19-29, 93-4; Jewish
immigration into 96, *see also*
under British Mandate, Israel
and Jerusalem; Jordan, unifica-
tion of Palestine with 63-4; land
ownership 62, 97-8; partition 36,
37-8, 40, 46, 106; population of
35, *see also* Jerusalem, demo-
graphical data on; *see also*
following entries and British
Mandate in Palestine
Palestine Commission 38
Palestine Conciliation Commission 38
Palestine Liberation Organization
148
Palmach 49
Patriarchs, Tombs of the 74
Paul VI, Pope 97
Peace Treaty, Egypt/Israel 114-16, 145
Peel Commission 36
Persia 23, 25, 155
Persian Gulf 149
Petahia of Ratisbon 95
Philistines 21, 23, 155
Pius XII, Pope 113
PLO (Palestine Liberation Organiza-
tion) 148
Pompey 24
Portugal 95

Ramsey, Michael 77
Ratisbonne 132
Reagan, Ronald 86
Red Cross, International 44, 70
Refugees 45, 55, 60-1, 63, 70-1, 83,
131, 147; repatriation of 62, 70,
126; *see also under* United
Nations Resolutions on
Jerusalem and Palestine
Reynier, Jacques de 44
Robinson, Rev. Edward 95-6
Rogers Plan 150
Rome 12, 24, 93, 155
Russia 28, 96

Sadat, President Anwar 114
Safed 96
St Saviour Church 74
Saladin 26, 114
Sanctuary of the Ascension 130
Security Council Resolutions on
Jerusalem and Palestine: **44** 39;
48 39; **187** 39; **237** 70, 83; **252**
83, 109, 124, 182; **267** 109, 124,

126, 183-4; **271** 109, 124, 185-6;
298 83m 125m 187-8; **446** 82, 125,
139, 202-3; **452** 109, 125, 204-5;
465 84-5, 86, 109, 125, 139, 145,
211-13; **476** 109, 125, 214-15; **478** 219;
for resolutions listed by subject
see United Nations Resolutions on
Jerusalem and Palestine
Selim, Sultan 27
Sephardim 13
Sheikh Bader 51, 132
Sheikh Jarrah 46, 51, 132
Shepherds Field 131
Shertok, Moshe 55, 106-7, 145
Sidetes, Antiochus 23
Silver, Dr 131
Sinai Agreement of 1975 148
Sinai Desert 69, 138
Solomon, King 22, 93
Solomon, Temple of 12, 23, 24, 26,
43, 73, 74
Sophronius, Patriarch 26
Spain 94, 95
Stern Gang 37, 50
Storrs, Ronald 13
Suleiman the Magnificent, Sultan
28, 49
Sykes-Picot Agreement 28
Syria 23, 33, 34, 69, 155

Talbieh 51, 132
Tel-Aviv 51, 59, 61, 110
Tell El-Amarna Tablets 20
Temple Mount 74
Terrorism 37, 43-5, 48
Thalman, E. 73-4, 75
Tiberias 25, 96
Titus, Emperor 24
Tours, Grégoire de 94
Transjordan 33-4; *see also* Jordan
Truman, President Harry S. 110
Trusteeship Council 45, 56, 57, 104,
105, 108, 147, 164, 165, 176-7
Turks in Palestine 26, 27-8, 29, 103,
156

UNESCO 76, 197-8
United Kingdom 28, 29, 46, 111;
see also Balfour Declaration,
British Mandate in Palestine
United Nations: Charter of 121, 143;
condemnation of Israel's annexing
of Old city 72; condemnation of
spoliation of Jerusalem by Israelis

76; Israel's assurances to 58-9, 60, 61, 107, 175; Israel's colonization of occupied territories, inquiry into 82; Jordan's occupation of Old city and 50; Palestine, discussion of question of in 1947 37-8; Palestine, Mediator for 40, 51, 55, 62; *see also following entries and* General Assembly Resolutions on Jerusalem and Palestine, Human Rights, Commission on, Security Council Resolutions on Jerusalem and Palestine, UNESCO, UNRWA, UNSCOP

United Nations Resolutions on Jerusalem and Palestine: demographic changes in Jerusalem 139; Holy Places 145, 161-2, 168-9, 172, 176, 185, 212; human rights and violation of by Israelis 59, 71, 162-3, 189, 191, 194, 201, 208-10; international régime for Jerusalem 56, 57, 104-9, 111, 161, 164, 171-4, 176-8; Israeli occupation 122-5, 138, 199-200, Postscript; Israeli withdrawal of armed forces from occupied territories 181-2, 206-7, 216-18; Jerusalem, status of 56, 104-9, 123, 124-5, 138, 139, 145, 178, 179, 182, 184-5, 187-8, 195, 202-3, 214-15; occupied territories 192-3, 195, 196, 211-13, 216-18; Palestinian rights 206-7; partition of Palestine 39, 106, 160-1; refugees 62, 63, 122, 145, 171-4; settlements in occupied territories 83-5, 138, 149, 150, 190, 201, 204-5, 211-13; *for listing of resolutions by number see under* General Assembly Resolutions on Jerusalem and Palestine *and* Security Council Resolutions on Jerusalem and Palestine

United Nations Truce Supervision Organization 69

United States of America 37-8, 84, 85-7, 110, 111-12, 137-40, 143, 148-51, 221, 222

UNRWA (United Nations Relief and Works Agency for Palestine Refugees) 71, 147

UNSCOP (United Nations Special Commission on Palestine) 38

Urban II, Pope 26

Versailles, Treaty of 33
Via Dolorosa 11, 157
Virgin, Tomb of the 130, 157

Wadi Joz 132
Wailing Wall 12, 35-6, 75, 76, 157
West Bank 69, 82, 83, 116, 138
Woodhead Commission 36

Yamin Moshe 132
Yost, Charles W. 112, 115

Zion, Mount 49, 74
Zionism 12-15, 29